Meeting by Design

Harnessing the potential of the web to revitalise meetings

Michael Clargo

TESSERACTS

Meeting by Design

Harnessing the potential of the web
to revitalise meetings

ISBN 9 780954 302146

First Published 2012 by Tesseracts
www.tesseracts.com

Meeting by Design

courtesy wordle.net

Executive Summary

The most pressing question facing chief executives today is, 'How do I engage the practical creativity and resourcefulness of my people to bring about a step change in performance?' and the fact is, for the vast majority of organisations, their current approach to meetings is a major obstacle to what they are trying to do.

The very high levels of ineffectiveness in meetings not only consume an undue proportion of management time (time which could be better spent on strategy, coaching, and business development) but it disengages and demotivates staff and actually supresses and misdirects the creativity and resourcefulness they are seeking to access.[1]

The potential of meetings to align our people with the right priorities, to develop their skills and attitudes, and to develop an inspiring and creative culture is far greater than most people realise. Sadly, this lack of realisation means that meetings are

[1] Extensive references to support all of the statements in this summary can be found in the relevant chapters, but have been omitted here to maintain brevity.

rarely constructed to fulfil their potential, and are more than 50 per cent ineffective in most organisations.

In large part this is because we do not treat meetings as a process, and we often select inappropriate tools within them. Furthermore, since meeting performance is rarely measured, most management teams are largely oblivious to the full extent of this issue. Conversely, expertly facilitated off-site workshops are often more successful in achieving the strategic, cultural, and operational shifts that are needed, precisely because they do recognise and embrace process, and because their effectiveness *is* measured and evaluated.

But the situation of routine meetings is mired in a range of established patterns and many years of habit, and is not so easily changed. This is especially evident in attempts to shift meetings to the web-based environment.

Ironically, web-based meetings not only represent the nadir of meeting performance, they are also the impetus and opportunity to transform it. Rather than simply import what we currently do in physical meetings into the web-based environment, we need to recognise the differences in the new medium and exploit these differences to address the issues that lie at the core of our meetings culture.

There are a number of easy, effective, and economic ways of doing this. Developing web-based meetings to be an *effective* alternative to travel is an 'easy sell' which establishes the need for change in current practice, but the techniques that are introduced in this way will establish new appreciation for meetings and, once proven, will be imported naturally into our physical meetings.

Key to making all of this work is for the executive to grasp responsibility for measuring and managing performance and progress, initially in the effectiveness of web-based meetings (which is relatively easy) and subsequently in the effectiveness of meetings overall. Doing so is not only likely to save your organisation half of its current travel costs, but will also double management's effectiveness in engaging their people's creativity to deliver a step change in performance.

Contents

Preface

An apocryphal story

Small Player Ltd, a small subdivision of Giganticus Inc., prides itself on its innovative approaches to collaboration. Two directors in particular, Paul Mangren and Barni Kyosa-Sha, have been hugely successful in inspiring their people to experiment with forms of meeting design, to inspire more energetic and enthusiastic participation. The results have been transformational.

Not everybody is a fan however, and they have come up against strong resistance, most noticeably in a recent health and safety audit, where the visiting auditors have been demanding the reinstatement of what might be seen as more traditional seating arrangements, forcibly arguing that 'unless the approved chairs and tables are used in the prescribed way, you cannot pass the audit!'.

Understandably, this brought Paul and Barni into sharp dispute with the auditors and, as a result, Paul and Barni have been asked to take the issue up with the Giganticus Board.

The Board meeting takes place of an afternoon, and so Paul and Barni had the opportunity in the morning to present some of their experiences to colleagues in HQ, who proved unanimously enthusiastic.

At 3.30p.m., Paul and Barni were welcomed by the Board, and explained some of the results that had been achieved, presenting figures and illustrations to support their case. However, at the end of their presentation, Joan Fass, the VP responsible for conformance, stood up and said, 'Standard meeting practices must be observed in order to comply with our submission for ISO 18005; all such meetings must be conducted only within the approved facilities and according to approved practices'. This spurred a number of intense debates in the Board.

After much discussion, the Chair, Petra Jones, stood up and addressed the whole group: "Colleagues, can you remember back to when we started this organisation? Do you remember how exciting it was? Do you remember our energy and enthusiasm to make a difference? Do you remember how it felt?

'This afternoon, we have heard stories of that same passion wonderfully infecting and informing the hopes of our staff, just as it did us.

'So, why are we trying to challenge this with burdens of bureaucracy that we never had to bear? We were inspired by the immediacy and proximity of making a difference, just as they are.'

The management team became silent again, as Barni and Paul explained in more detail the stories of changing mindsets, new ideas and inspired commitment to bring about transformation. When they had finished, Jim Stormsson spoke up: 'Friends, your attention for a moment please. Petra has eloquently reflected how many of us have come to a real love of our part in making this organisation what it has become. And I can remember back to one of our earliest meetings, when we were just beginning to turn this organisation around, and Dave Selznick, our founder, wrote how wonderful it would be if he could just capture what we felt then, and share it out to everybody we recruited. Do you remember that? Promoting an inspired way of working together is written clearly into our charter, and nowhere does it say that the only way we can keep our staff safe and healthy is to channel them into boredom and drudgery. I propose that we do everything we can to not put barriers in the way of our staff developing a passion for our business, but instead we should rethink how to embrace the essentials of ISO 18005 within Paul and Barni's approach.'

The whole meeting agreed this sentiment, and actions were set for guidelines to be drawn up and disseminated. Two members of the Board were tasked to work with Paul and Barni to spread their approach more widely and further promote engaging staff in this way, together with new guidelines to ensure their compliance with key standards.

A question to ponder

This meeting took place, but the precise topic and some of the words have been changed. If you could only base your answer on the form of the meeting – its structure and its flow – what would be your best guess as to *when* it took place?

Would it surprise you to discover that most people struggle to answer this question?

Introduction

The single, predominant, all-consuming question facing chief executives of Western organisations today is: 'How do I engage the practical creativity and resourcefulness of my people to bring about a step change in performance?'

The West no longer has a monopoly on the most advanced technology, and for many years it has ceased to be the cheapest place to access labour and resources, it is neither the biggest market nor the biggest supplier, and its statutory (and customary) overheads are growing increasingly expensive. At present, the only real edge that it has is its people, their experience, and their ideas, and even that is being eroded.

So whether we are talking about a competitive edge through effective strategies, reduced costs, better products, faster problem solving, or increased customer satisfaction, the question that *should* be facing managers in each of these areas is the one above. Is that not what your management is about? Whether these people are at the top of your organisation or the coal-face, whether they are in sales or delivery, whether they are technical, clerical or interpersonal, is that not what your leadership is about?

Because if your organisation is based in the 'more affluent' regions of the world, and if your management and your leadership are not inspiring your people to work together to quickly identify the best way forward (even if that way forward contains novel steps within it), then you are fighting a battle that you ultimately cannot win. No matter how hard we work our people we can never be the cheapest; no matter how controlling we are, we do not have a fixed prescription for success; the only battle we are capable of winning is one in which we can maximise our firepower, and that firepower is the wit, insight, understanding and ingenuity of our people.

But what about your meetings? How well are they designed to support this? How well do they engage the practical creativity of your people to bring about a step-change in performance?

It may seem strange to talk about meetings in this regard; it is almost incongruous that in one breath we expound the need for creativity and insight, and in the next we ask about meetings. And that fundamentally is the problem, and the reason this book has been written.

Meetings are an essential part of working life. To some, meetings are an essential evil; to others, an essential means of communication; to a few, they are an essential stage – a place for self-promotion. Unfortunately, the essential nature of meetings and their ubiquitous place in organisations leads us to take them largely for granted. Meetings are a Cinderella activity; an event of unrealised potential; an easily disregarded step-sibling of two other much more prominent aspects: leadership and management.

'Leadership' and 'management' clearly have the limelight in the pursuit of the 'glass slipper' of popular interest. The last three months have seen 5,000 new book titles in these areas,[1] but less than 2 per cent of these have been about meetings. And while literary contributions to leadership abounds with titles inspiring us to become a 'Leadership Powered Company', or to 'unlock its potential', and use words like 'soul', 'transformation' and 'charisma', the meetings list appears far more mundane. In fact, at the time of writing, search engine listings are headed by a book by the title of *Death by Meeting*.

The past few decades have seen a rapid increase in research and development invested in leadership:[2] some of it into the psychology of leadership, some into anthropology, and a lot more into consultancy and training to change the way that we do 'leadership'. Conversely, it is difficult to identify exactly when meetings last underwent a fundamental overhaul. Take, for instance, the short story in the preface. It is actually a piece of fiction. No such meeting has ever been recorded, well not in a book *about* meetings anyway. There *was* an almost identical meeting which took place on a different topic, but including that topic would give you a very good idea as to the date of the meeting. And the challenge of the preface is to identify, using just the nature, form, structure, and flow of the meeting, exactly when it took place.

[1] Source: Amazon.co.uk search engine.
[2] Source: Wikipedia entry on 'Leadership Studies'.

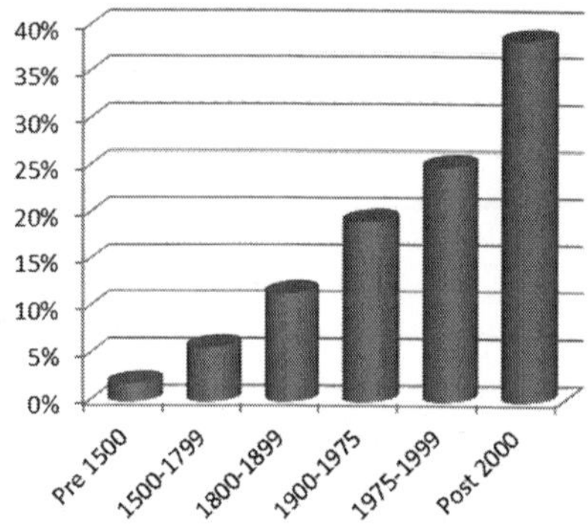

Most people struggle with working out a date for the meeting if they cannot rely on the names or the topic for clues (the graph on the right shows the range of guesses from senior managers). The point being made here is that, if you disguise the topic under discussion from the transcript of most meetings, it is difficult to tell from form alone whether they took place yesterday, last year, in the seventies, or even back in the nineteenth century. The reason for the difficulty in dating meetings on form alone is that their structure and nature has remained largely un-changed for generations. Over the last 50 years, our management thinking has shifted from 'task breakdown', through 'process thinking' to 'organic evolution', and our leadership has progressed from 'autocratic' and 'command and control' through to 'empowerment and participation'. But throughout this time our meetings have stubbornly remained predominantly 'show and tell', and 'chaired debate'.[1]

Before we risk any trivial bemoaning of a relative unfairness in different levels of progress, we perhaps ought to state why this differential rate of progress is an issue; why it matters that meetings have not evolved in the same way as leadership and management. The explanation for this is perhaps best illustrated by a question:

How are 'leadership' and 'management' delivered in practice?

---

[1] Source: Survey data further explained and expanded in Chapter 3.

Are not leadership and management predominantly delivered in meetings: formal or informal, group based or one on one, face to face or via technology, in different settings or at a distance? Is not the essence of leadership the influence of one person on others? And is not that influence most commonly effected through some sort of meeting? The pie chart on the right would indicate so;[1] it shows that almost 50 per cent of management time is committed to formal meetings, and a further 18 per cent in informal meetings.

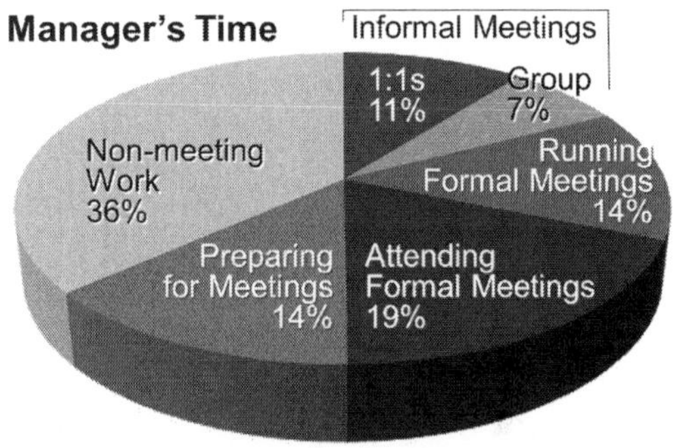

To be blunt, our understanding of the crafts of management and leadership have moved on, but the primary tool for effecting that craft (meetings) has remained the same, antiquated and tired, and largely incapable of 'engaging the practical creativity and resourcefulness of our people to bring about a step change in performance'. In fact they are sometimes a barrier to it.

And we have not noticed. We largely take the way we meet for granted, and virtually nobody questions whether there might be a better way (except to ask whether we can do less of it), and it has remained that way for literally millennia. If you turn to an example of a meeting in an old book, for instance the Bible, you will see that while the topics and the form of words may have changed, the structure remains very familiar to us. To illustrate

[1] Based on surveys across over 59 organisations, including multi-national, small commercial, public sector and charity. See Appendix 1, reference point A.

this, you may be interested to discover that if you open a Bible, and turn to Chapter 15 of the book of Acts, you will find an almost identical meeting to the one written in the preface; the form of meeting that many people dated within the last decade is actually almost 2,000 years old.

The issue is that meetings are traditionally a single-channel process. Only one person can typically (or more accurately 'politely') transmit at any one time, unless it is in the form of facial expressions or body language. This approach is well adapted to 'command and control' leadership styles, since it is relatively easy for a powerful person to dominate the flow and determine patronage within it, but it has a number of shortcomings in support of more participative and empowered leadership approaches. There are ways in which they can be adapted to be more facilitative, but these rarely happen in practice, and as a result the following issues are commonplace:[1]

- Lack of input from more reflective members of the meeting
- Domination of air-time by more forceful opinions
- Dismissal of creative opportunities through easy criticism and sometimes point scoring
- Reduced listening as people focus on seeking an opportunity to interject
- Repetition of arguments, because people feel they were not properly heard

To address these issues, it is common now for organisations to use facilitated off-site meetings for some of their most important

[1] Extensive data on these issues and their implications for organisation performance is included in Chapter 2.

decisions (albeit only perhaps annually). Many of these meetings are more multi-channel in nature.

Multi-channel meetings involve extensive use of wall templates, sticky notes, physical positioning, and other devices to engage people, inspire their creative insight, and enable them to communicate concurrently. In a multi-channel meeting it is rare to see people reading body language, because they can see the relevant input directly, and it is almost unheard of for someone to contribute nothing. Furthermore, creativity, consensus and commitment are commonplace. But sadly these meetings also have a number of drawbacks:

- A larger facility with different seating arrangements is needed
- It takes time to physically prepare, set-up, and take down the meeting's content
- Transcribing that content into notes is notoriously difficult
- Managers often lack confidence in leading such meetings.

And so the current balance is maintained. Multi-channel meetings are more productive but are expensive in time and facilities, and therefore fairly rare. Single-channel meetings are far less productive due to a number of issues, but are the only practical option for the vast majority of meetings.

But all that is about to change.

For the last decade, we have been standing on the edge of a technological and cultural revolution that will make multi-channel meetings far easier, more effective, and less time consuming in set-up and preparation. And it will mean that they can be held in virtually any room, of virtually any size and shape. It is a revolution that will affect every one of us, and many managers have already begun to engage with it.

This revolution is of course web-based meetings (although admittedly it does not feel much like a revolution at present). The revolution is that the ability to access multi-channel meetings now sits on the desk of virtually every member of staff. We carry it with us in briefcases and in our pockets. The functionality available to us through web-based collaboration addresses every one of the issues that beset multi-channel meetings. The features available to us through tools like Live Meeting, WebEx, and GoogleDocs enable us to plaster the walls of virtual meetings with templates (we refer to them as iFrames in the virtual world) of any size, to provide the means for everyone to engage; to contribute and 'listen' at the same time, inspire new levels of creativity, understand the balance of opinion quickly, reach consensus easily, and to build real commitment to the outcomes. In short, currently available web-based collaboration technology enables us to transform our meetings to be consistent with our long held aspirations for our management and leadership approaches; to engage the practical creativity and resourcefulness of our people in bringing about step changes in performance.

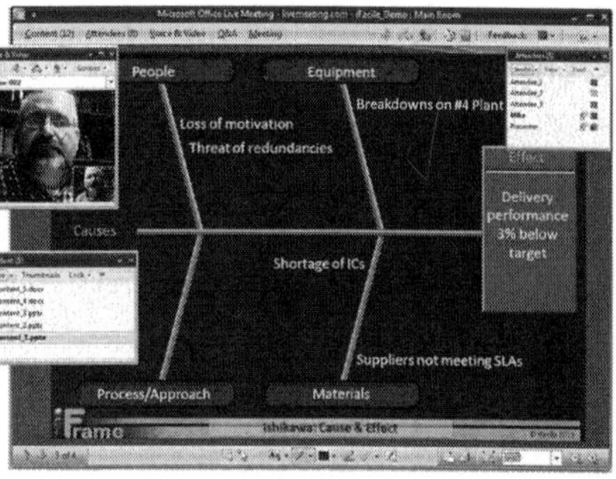

But the reason that it does not currently feel like a revolution is because, in practice, it is rare to find web-based collaboration being used in this way.[1]

It is somewhat ironic that, faced with this new opportunity, we simply try to adapt and force fit our current traditional (and deeply flawed) approaches into the new format. Virtually the only functionality that is accessed in most web-based meetings is the functionality you need for presentations and discussions[2] – a carry-over of 'show and tell', and 'chaired debate' – the techniques that have slowly evolved out of centuries of physical, face-to-face, single-channel meetings.

And as is alluded to on page 20, the only way in which to communicate if you are not the current single-channel is through body language and facial expressions, two things on which web-based collaboration is undeniably poor.

Faced with these challenges of transposing our current approach into the web-based environment, it would appear an excellent opportunity to reconsider our approach to meetings. But instead, it seems, we seek to find ways to make web-based meetings more closely resemble traditional face-to-face meetings, through better video and greater bandwidth,[3] an approach which is almost by definition destined to provide an inferior solution to physical meetings.

[1] Over 80 per cent of managers running web-based meetings were entirely unaware of a number of key elements of the functionality available to them, over 40 per cent were unaware of at least half of the available functionality. Survey data – see Appendix 2, reference point U.

[2] Survey data – as above

[3] 'Telepresence gains widespread use' listed as one of 'The Top 15 Technology Trends EA Should Watch: 2011 To 2013', Leganza, Forrester Research, 2010.

And what is the cost for this headlong struggle to maintain our current paradigm of meetings? Instead of everybody having immediate and inexpensive access through their PC or phone (desk-based or mobile) the new facilities take up entire meeting rooms, cost six figures in installation,[1] and are therefore rationed and need to be especially booked.

Why spend this sort of money on something that inevitably has to be inferior in its mimicry of a physical co-located meeting? It is not that 'better video' is a bad thing – indeed, improvements to see all of the meeting participants is a welcome development – but not at the cost of key functionality and convenience that could make meetings far superior to our current experience of physically co-located meetings.

Large format video conferencing facilities do have a compelling business case. Despite high cost of installation, each facility has the potential for 47 per cent ROI or more.[2] But it is the wrong business case. To illustrate this, imagine that you are a farmer back at the age of the horse and cart, and somebody brings you a modern truck. Large format video conference suites are akin to replacing the front grille with proper harness mountings, and for fitting a bench seat in place of the bonnet. It utilises the extra volume available but ignores the potential of the state-of-the-art internal combustion engine. The use of large format video conferencing utilises the bandwidth available in modern technology

[1] Estimated cost $300k per Telepresence suite, from 'Telepresence vs. Videoconferencing – Resolving the Cost/Benefit Conundrum', Wainhouse Research, Jan 2008.

[2] 'The ROI of Telepresence', Forrester Research, Feb 2009.

but largely ignores the potential of that technology to transform the way meetings actually take place.

While it is therefore clear that large format video does have a business case, it is a business case that fails to realise the different forms of interaction that are made possible through the web. Telepresence meetings will provide a saving, but improved use of web-based meetings can provide a bigger saving *and* improve organisational performance.

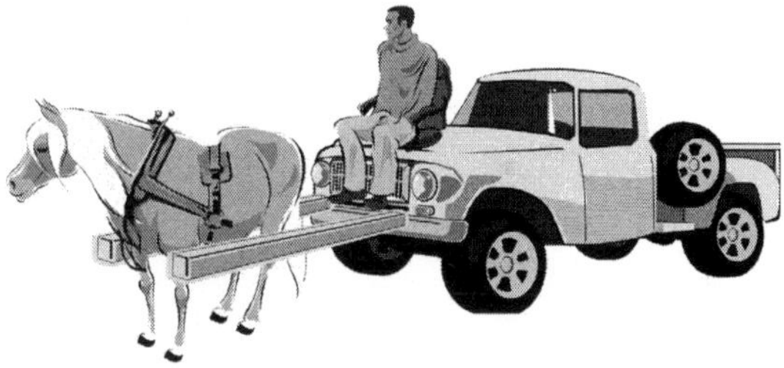

'Overall, I think I preferred my old cart, but you have to keep up with the times, don't you?'

Moving from traditional meetings to properly run multi-channel meetings (albeit web-based) has business[1] benefits in its own right. The fact that there are direct financial savings to be made from doing so is a wonderfully serendipitous opportunity. The farmer needs to take driving lessons if he is to get the best out of his new truck, and the lessons cost money and time, but in the world of web-based meetings that money and time is a fraction of what we save by transferring some of our 'travel-to' meetings to the new format. The business case is clear and justifiable on travel savings alone,[2] and this may well be the

[1] While we have used the word 'business' in its obvious contexts of 'business case', 'business travel' and (as here) 'business benefits' we do not wish to imply any lack of relevance to non-commercial organisations, for whom these points are every bit as pertinent to their efficiency and effectiveness.

[2] The ROI for investing in proficiency in using web-based meetings (*c.*400 per cent) is explained in considerable depth in the section on The business case (page 100).

compelling argument that begins our journey to greater adoption of multi-channel meetings, but it will not be what ultimately sustains it, and as we grow confident in our abilities to reliably deliver from such meetings, we will see that the real business benefit will be increasing levels of energy, creativity and commitment.

Our work in researching meetings, both physical and web-based, has given us a wealth of statistics which illustrate everything that you have read to this point,[1] but it has also has given us insight into how best to reverse this perverse clinging to an inferior and antiquated practice, and to fully grasp the potential of meetings.

The purpose of this book is to help you 'realise' (in a practical sense and within your own organisation) the benefits and the amazing potential of multi-channel meetings, initially through engaging effectively with the full potential of web-based meetings and subsequently, through using this as a springboard, to transform your physical meetings into events which really do engage the practical creativity, resourcefulness, and commitment of your people.

But it is vital that we do not underestimate the influence of centuries of conditioning on the way we think, and so the book is deliberately structured into theory (Part One) and practice (Part Two).

We recognise that in doing this, we have created a risk that some readers may try to skip directly to Part Two. However, the issues surrounding meetings are not straightforward, and any solution that is going to prove itself sustainable will need to be adapted to

[1] See Appendices 1 and 2.

the special conditions of its (your) unique organisational context with care and insight.

In the same way we would not expect a doctor to skip lectures on anatomy, or an architect to avoid anything to do with structural analysis, it is crucial that we too fully understand the nuances of the problem before we attempt to do something about it.

- In Part One, we look more deeply into the real purpose of meetings, and the extent to which current practice fails to realise anything like their full potential. We also look at the range of developments that will affect the way we conduct meetings in the future, and at what best-practice can teach us about how we can make best use of this.

  Each chapter in Part One has an 'In short' section at the beginning to introduce the theme of the chapter, and a summary section at the end, followed by questions for reflection. These allow you to hold on to the context of each chapter as you progress through the book.

- In Part Two, we take a practical approach to looking at how we can achieve far better performance in web-based meetings. We look at the potential of the technology; how web-based meetings can be designed to achieve everything you might want from them; and how to manage the culture to ensure you get the performance you need. And then we look at how this learning can be applied back into physical meetings.

> *As with Part One, each chapter in Part Two begins with an 'In short' and includes a summary of the main points covered. There is also an 'Outworking' section, containing short practical tips on addressing these points within your own organisation.*

Throughout the book, information and survey findings are used to back up the points we are making. These findings can be found in the appendices: a contents list on page 211, and the full data online at www.meetingbydesign.org/appendices. The password to access them is MBDAPP.

Part One

Understanding the Issue

Meetings have been a problem for a long time, and attempts to improve them have been, on the whole, unsuccessful and unsustained, even though it is generally accepted that meetings occupy too much time, are often inefficient, and usually are not fully effective.

But the many attempts to solve the issues of meetings have been largely simplistic. We tend to think of meetings as obvious and straightforward, which in reality they are not, and as a result of our lack of understanding we try and simplify things even further, rather than look more deeply into what meetings are trying to achieve, and the dynamics within them, as we would with all other important business processes.

If you are looking for a quick fix to your meetings, leaping to Part Two for the practical answers to implementation will not help you. In fact nothing will, because nothing has, and it is time to wake up to this fact. In other words, if you are expecting a panacea, this book is not for you.

But, if you are willing to recognise that improving this essential, ubiquitous, interpersonal process, which is so pivotal to our success and so consuming of our time, requires a fresh approach; and if you are willing to accept that this fresh approach needs to be founded on a greater level of insight and understanding, then the first step is to really understand what the problems are, and they are not as obvious as we might assume.

In Part One we will look at:

- Reconsidering the assumptions concerning the role of meetings (assumptions that have been overwritten by decades of habit and conditioning) and clarifying the full purpose of meetings within an organisation – Chapter 1
- Understanding (through data and research) the extent to which traditional forms of meetings fulfil that purpose, and how you might validate this within your own organisation – Chapter 2
- How global and technological developments are both placing more demands on, and offering more opportunities for, meetings, and how these developments make it more important to differentiate between types of meeting – Chapter 3
- What we can learn from successful meetings, in order to develop a blueprint for success – Chapter 4.

Chapter 1

The Potential and Purpose of Meeting

In short

The quality of your meetings impacts not only the performance outcomes of your organisation but also the engagement, development, and cultural aspects within it. Failure to fully appreciate this fact will lead to weaknesses in each of these areas.

Meetings, whether formal or informal, physical or virtual, are the key mechanism for leadership and management in any organisation. They are places in which decisions are made, issues are addressed, policies are unpacked and applied. But more than that, they are places in which culture is reinforced (for good or bad), attitudes are developed, behaviours are normalised, and relationships are formed and built upon.

> 'Where there is much desire to learn, there of necessity will be much arguing, much writing, many opinions; for opinion in good men is but knowledge in the making.,
>
> John Milton, 1608–1674

For management and leadership, and all of the things which they represent to an organisation, meetings are the place where 'the rubber hits the road'. Collectively, meetings are the most important process in any organisation.

It stands to reason then, given their importance, that great care must be taken in defining the purpose and design of meetings. But that does not appear to be the case in practice (as we will discover in the next chapter) and as a consequence we regularly find that the efficiency of meetings drops off, and the workload of the management and leadership roles correspondingly increases, to the extent that 63 per cent of managers now fail to take their full holiday allowance, predominantly because of workload and deadline pressures.[1]

Paradoxically, despite the importance of meetings, their role and functioning have been largely taken for granted, and in some cases have been seen as an obstacle to doing work rather than a key means to enable and support it. People have almost ceased to see the real potential of meetings, and this is reflected in a limited, even stultifying, impression of their purpose.

So what is the potential of meetings?

In the rest of this chapter we will unpack four key areas for the potential of meetings:

- Ensuring we are 'doing the right things'. This is probably the most obvious purpose; the continuous definition and refocusing of activities to ensure we deliver what is needed to meet the opportunities of our organisation – both at a macro and a micro level
- Building commitment and teamwork to ensure that the people are working enthusiastically toward a common (or at

[1] '"Destination Desk" becomes the top resort as holidays lose appeal', based on a survey of 553 managers, Petrook, Chartered Management Institute, 14 June 2006.

least complementary) goal, and that their endeavours are not in conflict with each other

- Growing future potential. Meetings represent the most important aspect of on-the-job training for future management and leadership
- Reinforcing the values and culture. The way meetings are conducted, and what happens within them, *are* the values and the culture of the organisation, irrespective of what might be said on any posters or policy documents.

These four areas of potential, shown diagrammatically on the right, do not represent four different types of meetings; they are true for *all* meetings, of whatever nature. All meetings, however brief, have the potential to contribute to (or maintain, or sadly to detract from) all of these areas, if not entirely within the meeting, then certainly within the things they set in motion. Failing to recognise this fact in determining the purpose of our meetings leaves these things to chance, and chance is not a particularly efficient agent of delivery.

Now look at those four bullets again. Do they not strike you as being the key things that you are trying to achieve through your leadership? Are they not the root of effective management? And if the design of our meetings is inefficient in delivering these things, and if so much of our time is taken up in meetings, is it any surprise that our roles as managers and leaders are taking more and more of our time?[1]

If we want our meetings to be better designed to achieve these things, we must begin by being clearer about the objectives that meetings are to fulfil. What is the real purpose of meeting?

Doing the right things

Can we define one set of purposes for all meetings? Surely there are different types of meetings? We have meetings for planning, for review of progress and/or performance, for updating staff, for personal appraisal and development, for problem solving. We have board meetings, budget meetings, sales meetings, design meetings, production meetings, supplier meetings. Do they not all have different purposes?

At a detail level they do, but good design does not begin at a detail level. Good design begins at a level which can see the overall pattern of meetings; their flow and connectedness, because, at this level, purposes become clearer and inefficiencies more obvious. At this level we can begin to see that all of the meetings we have are fundamentally about aligning the reality of what we are delivering to the reality of what is needed. Sometimes this is at different levels in the business, sometimes it is for

[1] Around two thirds of workplaces (64 per cent) reported that managers and professional staff had more work to do in the same hours than three years ago (Source: 'The Third Work-Life Balance Employer Survey', BIS.gov.uk, Nov 2007). Furthermore, 90 per cent of executives now feel that they have to be accessible outside working hours ('No escape from the office', Execunet Survey, 2006), and 40 per cent of people suffer post-holiday stress as a result of things building up while they are away (Institute of Leadership & Management, 2010).

different time horizons, sometimes it is for different aspects of the business (e.g., customers, employees, information, product, finances, image) but essentially each meeting is about aligning what we are doing with what is needed through a series of practical questions *(and activities to address them)*:

1. Do we really understand what is needed (currently and going forward) and does our stated intent reflect a good answer to fulfilling/exploiting the opportunities and challenges therein?
   - *Understand the situation, its context, and its implications*
   - *Explore the issues and critical factors within the situation.*

2. Do all of our planned and scheduled achievements build up to ensure the effective delivery our stated intent?
   - *Identify solutions to resolve issues and improve the situation*
   - *Establish goals; shared standards of success/achievement*
   - *Agree strategy and plan out steps for its realisation.*

3. Is actual current practice happening and interacting in a way which gives us confidence in the fulfilment of our planned and scheduled achievements?
   - *Ensure teamwork: relationships/communication for success*
   - *Manage progress: review metrics and resolve deficiencies.*

An effective meeting, of whatever type, is essentially about adjusting things so that each of the above questions can be answered with a resounding 'yes'. This same fact is true whether we are developing a five-year strategy for the business or changing the operational set-up on a machine; whether we are selling software to a new client, or setting annual objectives for an accountancy clerk.

The sidebar on page 37 introduces two diagrams which help to understand exactly what we are trying to do with different types of meetings. The grid illustrates the extent to which our meetings all try to achieve similar things: We may give them different names, and they will concern different subjects, and each will have a different focus and emphasis within it, but at a fundamental level the pattern of meetings is based around a small number of common elements – it is only the topic that is fundamentally different.

Understanding this helps us to ensure that meetings of all types are focused and efficient. To the extent that what is actually happening in a meeting is concretely answering one of the three questions on page 35 (or actively turning 'no' or 'maybe' answers around to 'yes' answers) then the meeting is efficient. To the extent that the meeting has lost sight of these three questions, or is waffling around them in the absence of clear data, or is failing to actively change 'no' answers, then the meeting is inefficient. It cannot even effectively impact the other purposes of meetings described in this chapter if it is failing at this fundamental level.

There is much more to be said about the purpose of meetings, but we can better defer that to Chapter 6, 'Embracing Process'. There is however, one last point to be made about the purpose of meetings and the three questions on page 35, and that is that the answers may be influenced both ways. Although the general flow may be in the direction from needs through to achievement (and

Sidebar: Bringing clarity to what we are trying to do

The diagram on the right illustrates the three questions on page 35 as the interfaces in a 2x2 grid linking the reality of our operational trajectory to the reality of a target which gives it meaning, through our continuously evolving expectations for both (in terms of our plans and understanding).

Different meetings may emphasise different parts of the diagram, depending on their needs at a particular time, but as can be seen from the diagram below, while the title and the content of the meeting may differ, the main purposes within each meeting are based on certain key meeting aims, which can be combined in different ways to achieve the necessary outcome.

This diagram lists a range of different meetings down the left; ticks illustrate a high level of commonality between their usual aims.

Types of meeting / Meeting purposes	Q1 Needs		Q2 Plans			Q3 Practice	
	Understand situation	Explore issues	Generate solutions	Establish goals	Agree strategy	Ensure teamwork	Manage progress
Strategy & Planning	✓	✓	✓	✓	✓✓	✓	
Progress Review	✓	✓	✓		✓	✓	✓✓
Staff/Team Briefing	✓✓	✓				✓	
Coaching / Appraisal	✓	✓	✓	✓	✓	✓✓	✓
Problem Solving	✓	✓✓	✓✓	✓	✓	✓	
Board Meetings	✓	✓	✓	✓✓	✓		✓
Budget Setting	✓			✓✓	✓		✓
Sales Visits	✓	✓	✓✓	✓	✓	✓	✓
New Product Dev't	✓	✓	✓✓	✓	✓		
Production Meetings	✓	✓	✓	✓	✓	✓	✓✓
Supplier Review		✓		✓✓	✓	✓	✓✓

rightly so) alignment can justifiably take place in the reverse direction as well. Meetings can change the answer to 'yes' by also:

1. Influencing what is needed by helping people understand the implications, or stretching their vision of what is possible
2. Adjusting planned and scheduled achievements according to budget, resource and operational implications
3. Informing our models of success through real data and insight into relationships.

However, they are far more likely to do this if they maintain their focus on what they are trying to achieve in each of these three areas.

Building commitment

To this point in the chapter, we have concerned ourselves with the logical outcome of meetings; the necessity of coming out with the rationally correct conclusion. As was stated earlier, this is essential, and all of the other purposes of the meeting are built upon this, but it is not sufficient. Successful meetings also have an emotional component, and this is often more influential of the result than the rational component in ensuring commitment to the conclusions.[1]

> 'Strong reasons make strong actions.'
>
> William Shakespeare

There are many who erroneously believe that once a meeting has arrived at the 'correct answer' that is the end to the matter, and they then get frustrated and confused when

[1] 'Transforming Giants', Moss Kanter, HBR, January 2008 and 'Quality People Management for Quality Outcomes', The Work Foundation, July 2009.

progress on the actions is slow, excuse-ridden, and sometimes non-existent. But the only outcome a meeting can realistically have is in the resulting attitudes and behaviours of its members. The meeting does not change anything except words on a page, it is the subsequent actions and responses of those who are involved in the meeting that either realises those words in practice, or does something different.

The emotional engagement of people with the conclusions of the meeting is essential to the meeting's ultimate success, but this goes far beyond mere nodding agreement and has huge implications for the very process by which those conclusions are developed. It is the commitment of people that is key to progress, and that commitment can neither be assumed nor equated to a few simple nods (or even worse, silence).

Commitment is something which we tend to oversimplify into a polarised outcome – people either are committed, or they are not. But commitment is a far more complex beast than can be described by 'yes' or 'no', and sadly this is something that most meetings entirely fail to appreciate.

Perhaps we can illustrate this by the following. What do you think 'I am in full agreement that we should implement X next week' actually means? There are a number of potential interpretations in the box on the right of the next page.

This is a broad spectrum of possible interpretations, but on which ones would you bet even-money to ensure the implementation of X? Only half of them are at a level where we can be relatively confident that things will take place as intended, and sadly, this is not the half that 'agreement' normally infers.

Getting to the higher levels of commitment is entirely achievable within the potential and purpose of meeting, but it is usually dependent on a mixture of a number of factors illustrated on the facing page (not all of which have to be present, but there does needs to be a sufficient number of them).

Levels of Commitment?

- I will accept it if X happens?
- I will support somebody else doing X if I am called upon?
- I will do A, B, and C in support of X, providing I can fit it in with my other priorities?
- I will delay my other work to do A, B, and C in support of X, providing there are no hiccups or problems?
- I am determined to ensure that I do A, B, and C, and will address any problems that occur?
- I will ensure A, B, and C happen, and go as far as D if it is needed for X to be implemented?
- A, B, and C are taken for granted, and I will take personal responsibility, no matter what, for ensuring X is implemented successfully?

It should be noted that these things do sometimes happen almost by accident, and so progress does get made and actions do eventually get completed. But it should also be noted that it is far more normal in many organisations that delays occur and implementations falter as a result of issues in these areas.[1] In fact they are so common that managers almost treat them as inevitable and unavoidable, and tend to be almost cynical about approaches which advocate that there may be an alternative. But that is exactly what we *are* advocating (and in doing so we are standing against centuries of conditioning): that

[1] *Motivation Matters*, Cook and Jackson, CMI Report, 2005, and 'Employee Motivation', Nohria, Groysberg and Lee, HBR, July 2008

Sidebar: Factors in Ensuring Commitment

- People believe the conclusion is the right conclusion; and this normally means that they believe their own concerns, issues and ideas have been heard and properly addressed by what has emerged
- People have a clear picture of what they need to do in support of the conclusion, and the true implications of success, failure, and/or delay (including for them personally)
- People are confident that their abilities and resources are sufficient to ensure success in their part of the project, and that areas of risk have been addressed
- People are confident that the other parts of the project will take place as planned, and that their colleagues are also sufficiently committed to it; and this means that those colleagues' concerns, issues and ideas have been heard and properly addressed by what has emerged
- There is a sense of 'team' in what is about to take place, and an unwillingness to let the other members of that team down.

To the extent that these things are *not* true for you, what do you do when you encounter your first obstacle?

- Heave a sigh of relief?
- Use all your effort and creativity to overcome it?

these factors need to be a conscious consideration in the defined purpose of a meeting, and in its design.

In practice, this means that the meeting needs to be structured in such a way that people get a chance to participate in developing the conclusion (even if that only concerns its local implementation), to constructively raise and address issues, and to contribute their own ideas and experience.

Essentially, the task is one of constructing a series of ways that people can engage with the subject of the meeting such that the conclusion becomes what they really want to do; developing and harmonising their aspirations to the activities that will need to take place. This becomes even more important in situations where the participants in the meeting, and those that are required to implement the conclusions, come from a range of different areas, departments, or even organisations.

Growing future potential

Every meeting you have within your organisation has the potential to grow your people, their engagement, and their abilities through:

- Inspiring people's commitment and aspirations to seek to develop their potential to make a difference within the organisation
- Providing people with insight and understanding into the logical framework by which the organisation functions
- Modelling a logical and methodical process for making good decisions in a way that people can replicate for themselves

- Building confidence in people for making practical, constructive, and (when required) creative contributions
- Educating and familiarising people with a set of good influencing and communication behaviours
- Stretching people into new challenges which are suited to their current stage of development.

Or alternatively, each meeting has the potential to:

- Frustrate, build resentment and demotivate people
- Create an impression of the organisation and the way it functions as a 'black art', only accessible through experienced intuition
- Obfuscate the decision making process, either as another impenetrable aspect of that 'black art', or as something that is the preserve of 'seniors', or as an irrational step of faith
- Discourage contributions and all forms of creativity
- Model political and/or autocratic means of achieving a particular outcome as the only viable way
- Limit people's development only to what they currently do or to official 'training'.

Which of these potentials is realised by the meeting, and to what extent, is another very important aspect of the purpose of meetings and their design, but sadly it is rarely recognised as such. The result of this oversight is that in some cases people take far longer to develop the potential that they have for taking ownership of aspects of the organisation's performance, and in other cases they take control but by using approaches and behaviours that are not always helpful to the rest of the organisation.

The issue comes from how we think about situations that require a meeting. The common traditional approach is reflected in the

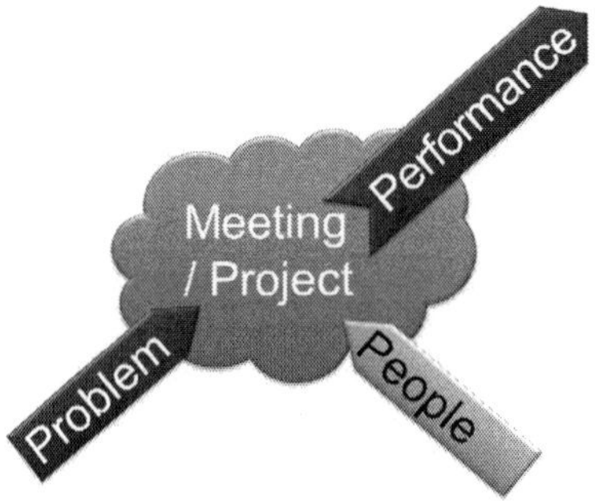

diagram on the left. The organisation encounters an issue or an opportunity, and it brings people together in order to address the issue and either restore or grow performance. Faced with this picture, the people who are selected, and the way that they are utilised in the meeting, are naturally optimised to be those who will have the biggest impact on restoring performance in the shortest possible time.

But the diagram only reflects half the equation, because while the people are working on the problem, the problem is also working on the people. If those people are established and experienced in such problems, there is very little work for the problem to do, and those people are likely to emerge from the experience very little changed from how they went in (except maybe a little more tired and worn down).

On the other hand, if we think about such situations according to the diagram on the right, and we begin to appreciate the way in which problems can develop the experience and potential of our people, we realise that every people/ problem combination has two

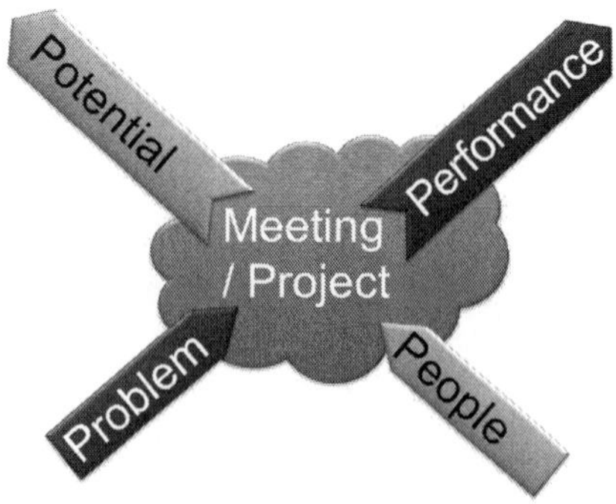

objectives: to improve the performance of the organisation for today, and to raise the potential of the organisation for further transforming performance tomorrow.

In reality, the selection of less experienced people to work on the problem is likely to result in a conclusion that does not achieve as much in performance terms as the engagement of a more experienced team, but it is important to bear in mind that we are simply talking about a 'less experienced' team, not an inept one, and what is being advocated here is a practical balance. Careful selection of the members, consideration around how the less experienced members may be coached, and good design around the process they will follow (meeting design) may well result in a small deficiency and/or delay in performance, but its contribution to the potential for future performance is huge; not only in terms of competence and confidence, but also in terms of motivation and productive relationships.

Reflecting back on the bullet points at the start of this section (page 42), good meeting design and participant selection has the potential to do all of these things efficiently and effectively, in a way that can transform the performance of your next level managers. It can:

- Model constructive ways to bring about change and motivate and enthuse people to engage with all such opportunities
- Illustrate and explain the intrinsic workings of the business in a way that brings deeper understanding and respect
- Educate people in effective and methodical practices for effectively fulfilling their responsibilities

- Draw out people's ideas and insights, and value them in a way which develops this insight and encourages them to contribute more...
- ...and to contribute in a way which also brings out the best in others
- Place upon them temporary responsibilities (both in and outside the meeting) which reinforces their learning in all of the above.

In other words, well-designed meetings are a way of teaching the 'next generation' of managers the true values of the organisation, and of equipping them to ensure those values are realised. And when we refer to 'engaging *more* of the practical creativity and resourcefulness of our people', we don't simply mean a greater proportion of those qualities, we also mean a greater pool of those qualities.

Reinforcing the values and culture

The true values and culture of your organisation are at a basic and fundamental level 'what happens in your meetings'. This fact is potentially the most overlooked by all those who seek to change their culture and values by means of lists of bullet points and phrases on posters and framed wall-hangings. Meetings are not simply a key contributor to the culture – they ARE the culture.[1] And if you want to control the culture of your organisation, you need to control its meetings; not just at the senior levels of the organisation, but all the way through to the 'coal-face'.

---

[1] *Corporate Cultures*, Deal and Kennedy, Addison-Wesley, 1982.

In part, this is illustrated by the contrasting lists of bullet points on page 42; from these it is easy to see how the quality of what happens in meetings influences the culture of the organisation.

But what we are talking about here is the deliberate design of meetings to reinforce the culture, and the setting up of simple non-bureaucratic controls to ensure that this happens in a positive way. The issue is that only in very few organisations are meetings 'in control'. To demonstrate this, please consider the following questions for your own organisation:

- How many formal meetings take place each month?
- What proportion of them are 'compliant' with any definition you have of values or culture?
- What proportion of them are seen as 'successful' in achieving their stated objectives?
- What proportion of the actions set in meetings are achieved successfully by the stated deadlines?
- What proportion of meetings fulfil participants' needs for participation, creativity, and confidence in the conclusions?

Given the amount of time that people spend in meetings, and the overall importance of meetings to the performance of the organisation, these are clearly very important pieces of data, and yet very few organisations collect this data and understand it for their organisation as a whole. And without this data, without these basic metrics of meeting effectiveness, meetings cannot be 'in control', and therefore neither can the values or the culture.

Does that really matter?

In the absence of any data, we could be forgiven for thinking 'probably not!'.

But in researching the material for this book we have taken the opportunity to collect data across a range of organisations. We have asked people to sample the meetings that they are involved in, and to collect data on various aspects of meetings, including the questions described above, and the results could well horrify those who do not already have an inkling about how the lack of metrics in managing meetings affects their performance. We will pick this up in more detail in the next chapter.

But before we do, let us take a moment to recap. Meetings have the potential to:

- Systematically harness the achievements of the organisation to meet the opportunity and challenges of its environment
- Build real commitment to ensuring effective progress
- Grow the potential of your people to face future challenges
- Establish your culture and values within the fabric of your organisation.

However, they rarely do so by accident, and to achieve these things effectively and efficiently requires that they are consciously considered within the purpose of the meeting, and that the process of the meeting is deliberately designed to achieve this purpose.

But maybe this is a step too far? Are meetings a process?

There are many who might have a psychological blind spot with this concept, not least because if meetings are a process then, in some way, we are a product of that process, and some of us might take issue with that idea, almost on a point of principle. We feel on safer ground when we think of commitment and attitudes, behaviours and relationships emerging naturally from events but the ideal of engineering them in some pre-determined scheme concerns us. If we see meetings as something we do to others, then we are concerned about the idea of manipulation, and if we think of them as something in which we too might be changed then our ego may feel challenged.

And yet, in a good meeting our attitudes *are* changed, otherwise conflicts could not be resolved, visions reconciled, or people developed, and we know that in a good meeting *all* of these things happen. And we know also of the events and interactions that enabled them to happen – not in some preordained manipulation, but as a consequence of being enabled to see context, possibilities, and other perspectives. Conversely we can almost certainly recall events in poor meetings in which the reverse of these things happened.

Therefore we can see that the patterns of what happens in meetings do affect their outcomes, and we can see that we too are influenced by those patterns. We can also see that the choice of different patterns of activity leads to different outcomes.

Because of these facts, it should be clear to us that meetings are a process, and that we therefore need to take responsibility for ensuring the right patterns lead to the right outcomes.

It is somewhat ironic that such thinking is almost taken for granted in our design of other processes within our organisations, and yet when it comes to meetings – the most ubiquitous, potentially powerful, and time-consuming of our organisation's management processes, it seems to be forgotten.

In summary

Meetings are the key process for leadership and management, but they are not recognised as such.

Understanding meetings as a process provides the potential to directly address many of commitment, cultural and development shortfalls, and thereby make more efficient and effective use of management time.

Part of our problem in facing up to this lies in an unresolved emotional response to the idea of being 'processed'.

Insight: Questions for reflection

To what extent do meetings in your own (part of the) organisation embrace their potential as outlined in this chapter? Do you know? Should you know?

To what extent do the other mechanisms your organisation has for doing these things really influence you and your decisions/ attitudes? Is this also true for others?

How have the points made on page 48 onwards left you feeling? To what extent is this entirely rational and does the emotional component carry any insights into the key things we need to resolve within ourselves if we are to make progress?

Chapter 2

The Parlous State of Meetings

In short

If half the meetings we undertook were better designed and facilitated we would not need the other half!

Please note: This section uses numbers within the text to reinforce key messages with real data. While this makes reading this chapter a bit 'bumpy', it has been a deliberate decision to do this and it reflects the importance we place on ensuring sufficient credibility for the reader to truly understand and appreciate the issues. We believe this is key to making progress.

Managers spend an average of half of their time in meetings, and a further 14 per cent preparing for them.[1] Meetings are the primary consumer of management time, and management time is an increasingly scarce commodity.

Furthermore, management effects the vast majority of its role through meetings: 91 per cent of formal meeting time is con-

[1] Survey averages: 33 per cent in formal meetings, 18 per cent in informal meetings, 14 per cent in meeting preparation and travel – see Appendix 1, reference point A.

cerned with planning, reviewing, problem solving, or communicating outcomes (see the pie chart on the right).[1]

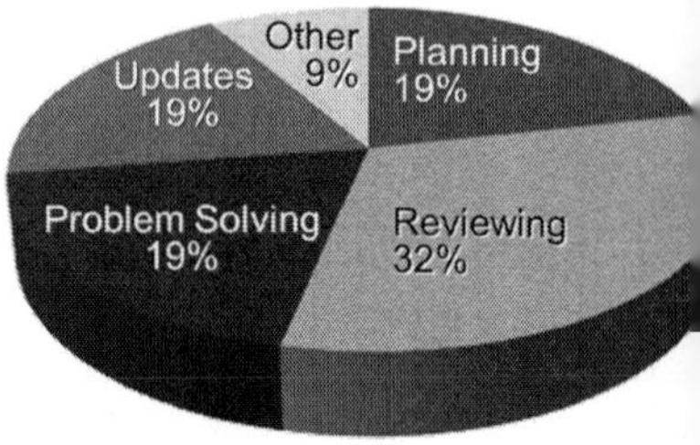

Split of meetings attended by managers

Since quality of management is the biggest factor by far in driving an organisation's performance, and since meetings are the primary process of such management, you might expect the meeting process to receive far more design attention than any other process. But you would be sadly mistaken.

Meeting performance is probably the least measured, least reviewed, and least improved of all organisational processes[2] and, as a result, managers have become stressed and overworked.

In this chapter we look at the consequences of this and its implications for how well our current approach to meetings fulfils the purposes we outlined in the previous chapter. In particular we will look at:

- Whether meetings are effective in driving business (or organisational) performance, or simply driving busy-ness
- The extent to which meetings ensure the commitment that is necessary to drive efficient progress
- The utilisation of people within meetings and the influence this has on their development
- How meetings impact the culture of the organisation.

---

[1] Survey averages – see Appendix 1, reference point B.

[2] Survey averages: almost 80 per cent of meetings are not reviewed by the participants or evaluated by metrics – from base data to Appendix 1, reference point H.

A drive to activity or achievement?

Not that long ago, meetings without a defined objective or an agenda were relatively commonplace. Fortunately those times are largely past us and there are now three times as many meetings with a clear and defined objective as there are without.

However, there are a number of issues concerning the quality of those objectives. The most obvious of these (see diagram on the right) is that only half of all meetings have defined their objective in SMART terms.[1]

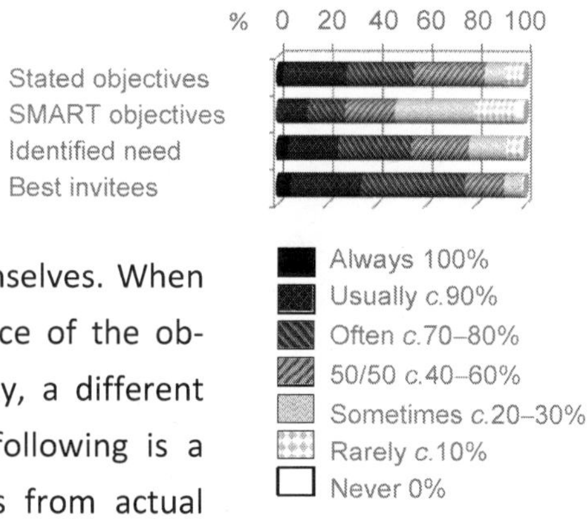

But a far bigger issue concerns the nature of the objectives themselves. When you look underneath the existence of the objectives to what they actually say, a different picture begins to emerge. The following is a sample list of defined objectives from actual meetings:

- Ship all products on-time
- Introduce new products in support of customer demand
- Review apprenticeships
- Interview an individual using a predefined set of questions
- Roll out new product to the field
- Document the project delivery process.

[1] The acronym SMART applies to objectives that are specific, measureable, agreed, realistic, and timely. Our survey question emphasised the first two elements of this in respect of meeting objectives: specific and measureable.

Apart from the first item on this list, how would you know whether the meeting had actually made a tangible difference to the performance of the organisation? And, providing each meeting fulfilled its objective, how would you know whether it had done so 'well'?

Based on our survey of actual meeting objectives, only 22 per cent of those submitted had an intrinsic quality by which it was possible to determine if the outcome had a positive impact, and only 6 per cent attempted any tangible quantification of that impact. The rest tended to reflect the simple completion of an activity as being sufficient.

The danger here is that activity-centric objectives tend to lead to a meeting structure which is simply about completing the activity, often without a full understanding of the real potential of that activity to impact business performance. In part, this is because the pressure on management time is such that there is little opportunity for meeting design and preparation, and so we begin to lose sight of the objective, and focus instead on the list of tasks that need to be completed.[1]

Sadly, in an environment where everybody is under pressure, and where the phrase 'more meetings' is rarely viewed in a positive light, the goal in meetings is often to finish as quickly as possible and move on. With a task-centric objective, in a time-pressured environment, the goal is to simply complete the task 'as defined'.

The way we undertake each task within an organisation has the potential to fulfil any of the four descriptions in the diagram to

[1] 'Stop Wasting Valuable Time', Mankins, HBR September 2004

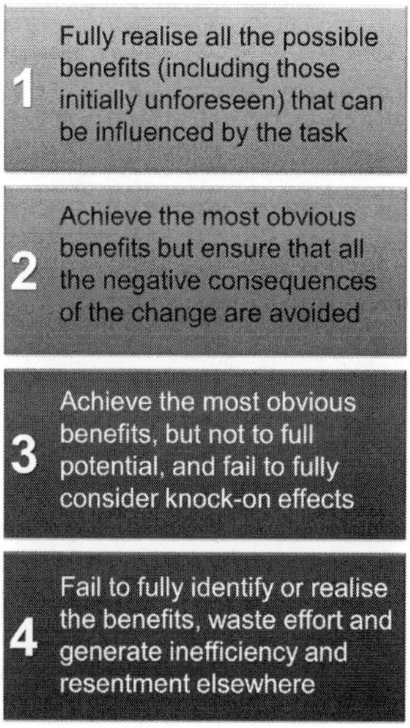

the right. If we describe a task purely in terms of its completion, then we permit the possibility of all four outcomes. In this situation, the most likely outcomes are 2 or 3. Rarely do we arrive at 1, and sadly there are many instances of 4, particularly in policy setting, quality procedures and systems projects.

The issue is that the overall performance objectives of our organisation stay the same, and every meeting has the potential to contribute to these significantly, slightly, not at all, or negatively. Failing to ensure the maximum contribution of our meeting to the achievement of our overall objectives generates more work for our-selves, which in turn puts us under more time pressure, which in turn means we have less time to develop good objectives and process for our meetings, which in turn means that they underperform, and so on (see sidebar on page 57). In a world of relentless demand for performance, where management time is so much under pressure, and at least 50 per cent of that time is invested in meetings, it may behove us to consider the following:

- Do we know what proportion of our meetings have a clearly defined linkage between their objective and the organisation's performance?[1]

---

[1] *Managing by Design*, Clargo, Tesseracts, 2002.

- Do we know how effective our meetings are (on average) at achieving their full potential impact on performance?
- Do we even know how many meetings it is taking us to achieve our performance?

While the logic expounded in the sidebar may be dismissed as a nice piece of theory, something that is not so easy to dismiss is the finding that 46 per cent of managers report that half or more of the meetings they attend would not have been necessary if preceding meetings had been more efficient and delivered what they set out to deliver (26 per cent say that 75 per cent of their meetings fall into this category).[1]

All of this inefficiency increases the total number of meetings that *are* necessary, and thereby the pressures on management time. But it is not just the attendees that end up rushing from one meeting to another, it is the people chairing the meeting as well, and as a result they lack the time to prepare and think through exactly what they are trying to achieve in the meeting, and the most efficient way to achieve it. This is borne out in the survey data: 55 per cent of meetings lacked an efficient process and 52 per cent lacked any form of clear timed agenda.[2] Further to this, where an agenda did exist, 41 per cent of meetings failed to stick to it.

It seems the parody of arrows on the facing page may not be sufficient to reflect the true depth of the problem, and furthermore it only reflects what might be seen as 'necessary' meetings.

---

[1] Survey data - see Appendix 1, reference point K.
[2] Survey data - see Appendix 1, reference point D.

Sidebar: Role of Meeting Efficiency on Management Time

Let us assume that we have defined our organisation performance targets for the year. And let us assume that if every meeting we hold is focused on achieving its maximum potential for impacting that performance, each meeting will contribute (on average) 0.1 per cent of our progress toward those performance targets. Then we can conclude that we will need 1,000 meetings of such calibre to achieve our targets.

But supposing that those meetings are not designed and focused to achieve their maximum contribution and because of this, they are only half as effective as they could be. How many meetings do we need then?

Or worse still, supposing those meetings had totally lost sight of their potential impact on the performance targets, and had become instead 'activity-centric'. How many meetings do we now need to ensure our performance targets are met?

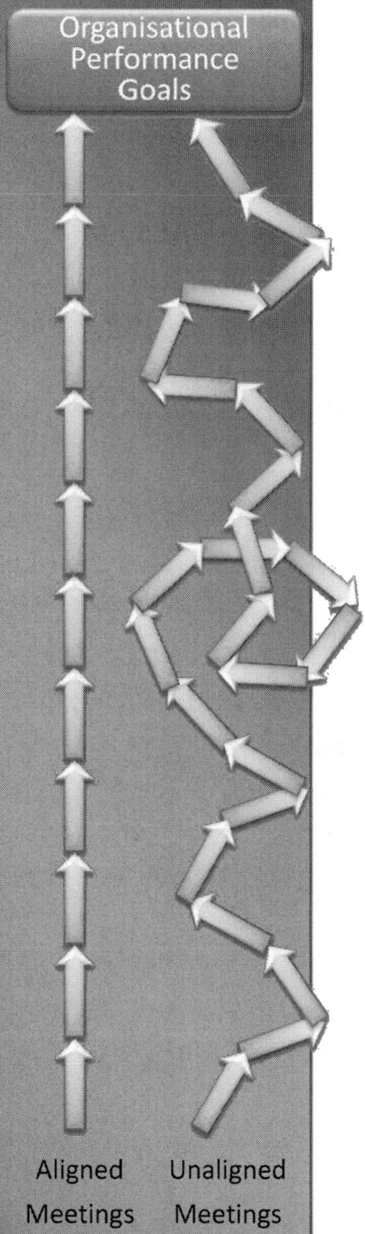

In response to the question: Was there a clear need for the meetings to take place at this time? (Rather than simply following an established pattern). The answer was 'no' for 39 per cent of meetings![1]

What we are seeing here is the outworking of a vicious circle: 1. The volume of meetings puts pressure on management time; 2. Management lack the time to properly plan their meetings; 3. The meetings become inefficient; 4. More meetings are required.

The consequences of '2. Management lack the time to properly plan their meetings' can be seen by revisiting the example list of objectives on page 53. To look at them, you might think that they had been developed in a vacuum, not in a tangible world of issues, opportunities, and shortcomings. Where are the quantified descriptions of deficits that need to be addressed? Where is the gap we need to close to reach our current aspirations? Where is the cost of the litany of issues that we need to resolve? Identifying and targeting good focused objectives for a meeting takes a degree of research,[2] but this tends to get short-cut when managers are under pressure – and, as a consequence, we continue the vicious circle and generate yet more pressure.

Tolerance or commitment to outcomes?

The issue of the quality of meetings is further borne out in people's commitment (or lack of it) to the outcomes. The issues thrown up in the preceding section clearly undermine the list of

[1] Survey data – see Appendix 1, reference point D.

[2] Even if it is only reviewing the data, and asking the relevant people what is going on? and what is needed? and why? and how that impacts the goals?

factors required to ensure commitment that we considered on page 41, in particular the purpose and value of the conclusion to the meeting, and also confidence in the commitment of others.

It may therefore be of little surprise that 45 per cent of meetings result in actions which people are not confident will be delivered to the agreed schedule, and that 60 per cent of organisations fail to deliver the energy, commitment,[1] and passion to move forward (and to deliver the actions) in half or more of their meetings.[2]

This of course has a knock-on effect on subsequent meetings, and we find that 45 per cent of meetings suffer from dependent actions not being completed in time. This corresponds with 48 per cent of all meetings failing to fulfil their original purpose due to a shortage of key information.[3]

The organisational response to this deficit in commitment and its implications for delivery of actions is to *hold more meetings*. These additional meetings are often termed progress reviews, and while their aspiration may be 'value-add': removing road-blocks, providing support, etc., the reality is often that they are more about chasing progress than enabling it. Sadly this is often a vital function, it is fairly common to see a flurry of activity to complete things 'for the meeting',[4] but the consequence of this is

---

[1] The issue of commitment was flagged up by the Chartered Management Institute, which found that 49 per cent of managers do not feel positively motivated. 'Survey into Quality of Working Life', Worral and Cooper, CMI, 2007.
[2] Survey data – see Appendix 1, reference point J.
[3] Survey data – see Appendix 1, reference point F.
[4] 'Completion of actions is a problem in that it's usually obvious that people either haven't done them or have done them hurriedly at the last minute. It also seems that actions are not always recorded accurately, and people don't clarify or challenge the inaccuracies until the next meeting.' Quote from respondent to survey – see Appendix 1, facing reference point G.

that 39 per cent of meetings only exist because people do not do what they say they are going to do.[1]

As a result of all this, participants feel that their own time is used well in only 53 per cent of meetings, which is a little bit better than their estimate on the effective utilisation of their colleagues' time (51 per cent).[2]

These figures may well shock and horrify you, but that may be because we are reporting on meetings in a way which is very uncommon. Most meeting reports within an organisation tend to be anecdotal, delivered by the meeting organiser who can sometimes hold an optimistic perspective on what they *hope* has been achieved. (In the absence of any evidence to the contrary, people tend to incorrectly assume that their *own* meetings achieve what they set out to achieve.) The data you are looking at here are more quantified and from the perspective of the meeting participants, who are often more realistic about what has actually been delivered. Sadly this vital data is rarely collected or analysed, and as a result the issues continue largely unchecked.

Consumption or development of talent?

The diagram on the facing page is a redraw of the potential for meetings to develop talent within the organisation that we first explored on page 42. In light of the findings of the preceding sections, the ideal behind the description on the left hand side of the diagram may now seem somewhat distant.

[1] Survey data – see Appendix 1, reference point K.
[2] As above.

But what about the other aspects of developing and utilising potential, particularly in respect of 'engaging practical creativity and resourcefulness'?

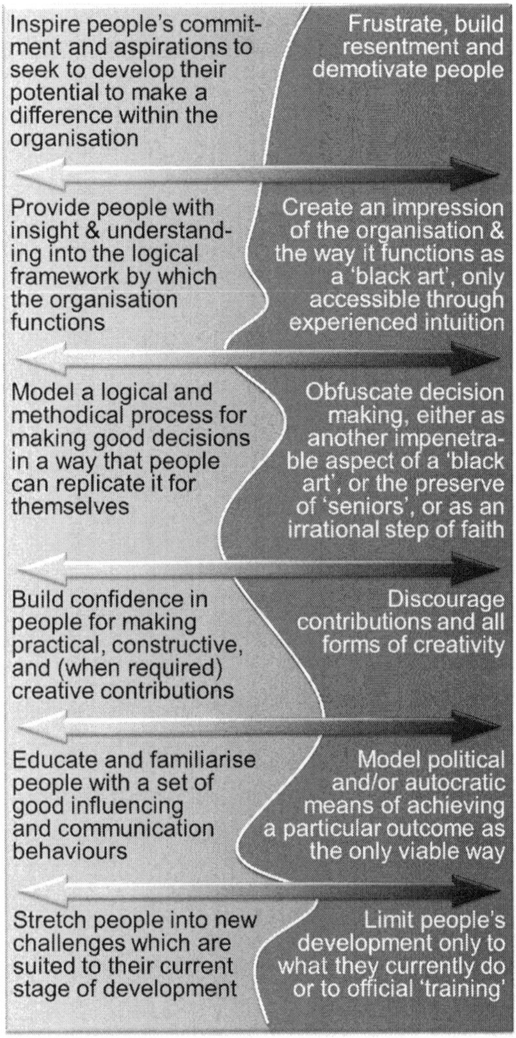

To explore these we surveyed organisations on a number of aspects regarding what happened within their meetings.

In respect of 'providing logical insight and understanding into the logical framework by which the organisation functions', we discovered that in 56 per cent of cases, useful pre-reading was not available prior to the meeting, and even when it was available, it was often not accessed by people attending the meeting.[1]

Furthermore, 60 per cent of organisations rarely or never utilise findings from relevant external literature (papers and periodicals) within their meetings, in respect of current innovations and best

[1] Survey data – see Appendix 1, reference point F.

practice (nor indeed in the pre-reading for those meetings).[1] It seems that managers are rarely exposed to such resources, particularly within the operational context of meetings, and are therefore denied a useful source of insight into the theory of their organisation and lack the opportunity to consider a range of contrasting approaches to the work at hand – insight which could usefully influence their decision making. This omission has two effects: The first, which is obvious, is that they do not get to utilise best practice insights; and the second, which is less obvious but potentially more damaging to the organisation, is that they do not get to value them.

With regard to 'exposure to a logical, methodical and replicable decision making process', 68 per cent of organisations rarely or never use problem solving tools within their meetings.[2] Sadly, this reflects a popular misbelief that problem solving is reserved to special types of meetings; a belief which is reinforced by the poor quality of objectives that are usually defined for meetings.

All organisations have problems. If an organisation does not have a problem, then its problem is that it is operating way short of its potential. When problems cease to exist, it is time to set more ambitious targets that better reflect the true potential of the organisation. These targets create gaps in performance between intention and reality, which then need to be solved. And as we reflected earlier, the role of meetings is to close that gap to achieve the target performance of the organisation. Closing such performance gaps (bringing about a step change in performance) is best served by processes which harness the insight and creativity

[1] As above.
[2] Survey data – see Appendix 1, reference point E.

of your people. Problem solving tools represent the most efficient and productive way of doing this.

However, while it is clear that problem solving tools are used far less frequently than they should be, this issue is dwarfed by the practical absence of creativity tools in meetings: 94 per cent of organisations use creativity tools rarely or never in their meetings.[1] Given that most manual labour and routine tasks have migrated from the West to low-cost countries, this represents a serious omission. All we really have left in developed countries to compete with in the global economy is our insight and our ideas, and if we are not regularly using the best tools to inspire and harness these then we are ultimately doomed to failure. Without a flow of innovation, discovery, and insight, what value do we actually represent in the global economy?

Finally, in terms of how well we stretch people into new areas of challenge, which reflect their current stage of development, 61 per cent rarely or never take account of people's development plans when setting actions in their meetings.[2]

Perhaps the issue in all of this is still pressure – pressure within the meeting rather than outside of it. We might expect 'new blood' to be inherently more creative, more exposed to new thinking and ideas, but developing new perspectives and new ideas takes thinking time; time for reflection on the problem. Furthermore, new managers are often more circumspect over expressing their views, and therefore like to take time to consider them more before introducing them to their more experienced

[1] Survey data – see Appendix 1, reference point E.
[2] Survey data – see Appendix 1, reference point K.

colleagues. Unfortunately, this time tends to be fairly rare in meetings, and it is common to find that those who are more vociferous (and often less reflective) in their opinions dominate the discussion. The consequences of this are a significant imbalance of involvement and contribution (an issue in over half of all meetings).[1] Sadly, despite a lot of good literature on participative leadership and facilitative management styles, the traditional process of meetings holds back the realisation of these principles to the extent that the prevailing management styles are still bureaucratic, reactive, and authoritarian.[2]

What we are seeking to emphasise here is not so much the idea that reflective managers are too diffident and bashful to say something obvious when it is clearly needed, but that they are unlikely to introduce the *beginnings* of a dawning realisation; a vague sense of disquiet or opportunity, the sort of idea which opens with the phrase 'It may be nothing, but a thought strikes me' and all of a sudden the meeting sees a brand new perspective that had previously been obscured from their view. If such perspectives are to be useful, they need to be timely, and that means that they are likely to be fairly raw and unformed when they are first voiced – they may even be seen as a distraction by the more 'driven' management styles in the room. In other words, the 'practical creativity' that executives are seeking from their people tends to be a fragile entity at the point when it is to be of most use, and sadly the survey data indicates that 60 per cent of

[1] Survey data – see Appendix 1, reference point G.

[2] The management styles reported as the most prevalent are bureaucratic (40%), reactive (37%) and authoritarian (30%), 'Survey into Quality of Working Life', Worral and Cooper, CMI, October 2007.

meetings are unlikely to benefit from any perspective that is not already strongly formed, and possibly even dogmatic.[1]

Progress through values or despite them?

This last point illustrates that the culture in most meetings may not be a culture which values all of the qualities which the organisation may aspire to. By the very nature of how the meetings take place in practice, they may value competitive, aggressive, charismatic, and 'shoot from the hip' characteristics to the cost of those that are empathic, analytical, creative, and insightful (see footnote 2, page 64).

Part of the issue is that many meetings have no defined standard of which behaviours they intend to promote and encourage, and 83 per cent of meetings lack any form of defined ground rules, or reference to them.[2] The lack of such a simple device means that the underlying expectations for the culture of the meeting are entirely subjective, and challenging 'unproductive' behaviours within the meeting becomes a lot more difficult.

And it is not just where the judgement of appropriate behaviour is subjective that there is an issue in meetings. Even behaviours which are objectively wrong are often not addressed. Despite the levels of problems in people failing to undertake appropriate preparation, and also problems with behaviours that were reported in the earlier sections of this chapter, 62 per cent of meetings tend not to follow-up on those who fail to prepare or complete their actions, and people feel that only in about 39 per cent

[1] Survey data – see Appendix 1, reference point G.
[2] Survey data – see Appendix 1, reference point D.

of meetings do they have any confidence that obvious behavioural deficits from participants in the meeting will be addressed offline. It is very common to *not* follow up (35 per cent see it as rare or never; 74 per cent half the time or less).[1]

The consequence of this is obvious, and the resulting, inevitable, continuation and impact of such behaviours are evident in the data presented throughout this chapter.[2]

In virtually any other process in any organisation, these performance statistics would not be tolerated, but with respect to the meetings process there is actually very little available to alert people to these statistics – 78 per cent of meetings lack any form of meeting review, and even where they are reviewed, those reviews are rarely used to guide subsequent meetings.[3]

Senior management is largely unaware of the performance issues in their meetings process – very few organisations have a consistent framework for reporting meeting performance back up the organisation. Furthermore, in the absence of such statistics, our propensity for self-deception is a big factor in our lack of awareness. Managers are largely oblivious to this trend in their *own* meetings and, for this reason, the survey deliberately asked questions about meetings people attended rather than those they chaired.

You may feel that your meetings are fine – virtually every manager does – but how then do we correlate this with representative

[1] Survey data – see Appendix 1, reference point H.
[2] Overall, six out of the seven factors cited as being the biggest influences in meeting inefficiency and ineffectiveness are behavioural. The seventh was meeting design. Survey data – see Appendix 1, reference point L.
[3] Survey data – see Appendix 1, reference point H.

data of those same meetings as perceived by others? Do *you* have the equivalent data for your own meetings and those of your organisation?

Self assessment

Of course, the data reported in this chapter are averages. They are gathered from a wide range of sectors, geographies, organisation sizes and types, and they are relatively consistent across these, but your organisation may be different. And while the uncertainty about whether your own organisation is an exception to these data remains, it will be difficult for you to persuade your organisation to definitively take action one way or the other.

The data presented in these pages may be a spur to action, but they should not be the rationale for it. Even if your organisation is consistent with the picture reflected here (and the probability is that it is) it will have different emphases within that picture, and these emphases will be key to defining an efficient programme of change which has the emotional and rational backing of your colleagues. It will also be key to evaluating and managing progress toward the meetings culture that you want to create.

The only practical answer to this is to conduct your own meetings survey within your organisation. To help with this, there are some basic guidelines to conducting a survey included as Appendix 3.

Within this appendix is a link to automated surveys which can be accessed over the internet. These are relatively inexpensive (and in some cases free) and enable you to undertake your own online survey within your organisation and receive a PDF report on the results.

In summary

Meetings in general fail to realise their potential. Many are undertaken with little forethought or preparation, and with limited, if any, consideration of what they might achieve or how.

On average, meetings are less than 50 per cent efficient, and this parlous situation is allowed to continue due to a lack of any objective measurement of meetings performance.

A failure to grasp the potential of meetings has led to an inability to effectively manage culture, and an impoverished approach to management development.

Insight: Questions for reflection

How do you feel your own organisation compares with the data outlined in this chapter?

Do you have objective evidence of the performance of meetings at different levels and in different areas?

What would the opportunity to halve the number of meetings release your people to do better?

Chapter 3

The Emerging World of Meetings

In short

Global, technological and social developments will have a big impact not only on how meetings take place, but on their very nature. We will either engage with this or be overwhelmed by it.

For centuries, meetings have been our key mechanism for collaboration, but the nature of collaboration is changing as never before, and with it, the concept of meetings is also being transformed.

No longer are meetings confined to one event, in one place, at one time. The potential that is now available blurs the boundaries and conventional limits of what we think of as a meeting. Meetings in this new world are not so much an event as a discipline, and it is now possible to hold meetings as multiple events, in multiple places and at multiple times if required,[1] or any productive subset within that – whatever is most effective and efficient for moving things forward.

[1] Meetings which take place at different times for different people are referred to as 'asynchronous' (i.e., not at the same time).

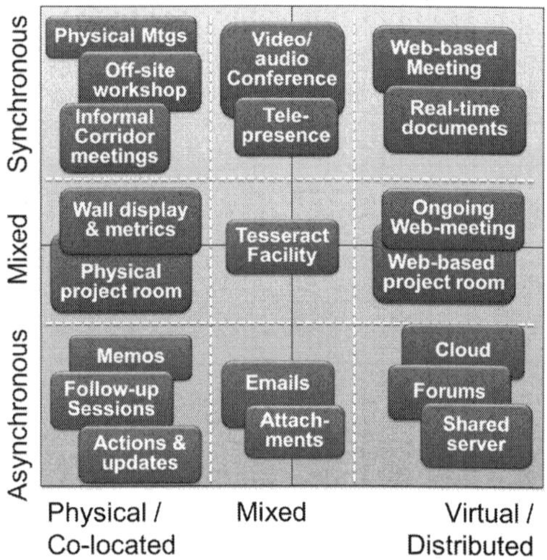

Whereas meetings were originally very much a product of the top left-hand corner of the diagram on the right, the forces at work in the world today encourage, support, and ultimately demand their migration into other areas of the chart.

In this chapter, we look at the implication of these forces for our practice of meetings:

- The impact of globalisation and distance
- The role of technology and the Internet
- The opening up of markets which are more economically placed to do what we traditionally do.

We also look at how these forces will drive us to more clearly differentiate between the meetings we need and the mechanisms we can best use to deliver those meetings:

- How meetings and learning need to become more closely aligned
- The idea of 'tag' meetings to handle routine communication
- The idea of 'tackle' meetings to inspire greater levels of commitment and creativity.

The impact of globalisation and of distance

The last few decades have seen tremendous growth in the geographic dispersion of people who need to work together,[1] and an almost equally large increase in the need for collaboration between those people who are geographically distanced.[2]

There are a number of factors behind this:

- The Internet has brought a viable solution to the practical globalisation of markets and thereby supported increasing numbers of international customer–supplier relationships and partnerships
- Competitive pressures have driven manufacture, and some service provision, away from the point of use to low-cost countries which may be half way around the world
- The opportunity for office cost savings has led to downsizing of corporate floor space and corresponding increases in 'hot-desking' and home-working[3]
- Increased levels of travel has led to people working away from their 'home-office' for significant periods of time.[4]

The image on the next page illustrates the extent to which globalisation now affects organisations; the numbers in the map represent billions of dollars per annum ($6.23 Trillion in total) in *intermediate* goods and services (that is, goods and services which are produced by an organisation in one country, and then need to

---

[1] 'Economic Globalisation Indicators', OECD, 2010.
[2] 59 per cent of the work done by management now depends on relationships which are 'at a distance'. Survey data - see Appendix 2, reference point Q.
[3] Over 25 per cent of the UK workforce now 'sometimes' work from home – Daily Telegraph, 7 February 2011.
[4] An average of 890 hours per year is now spent by managers in travelling.

be further worked on by an organisation in another country in order to produce their own products and services). The intermediate nature of these goods and services illustrates the growing interdependency that has emerged from exploiting global opportunities for best-cost, best-IP, or best-location solutions.

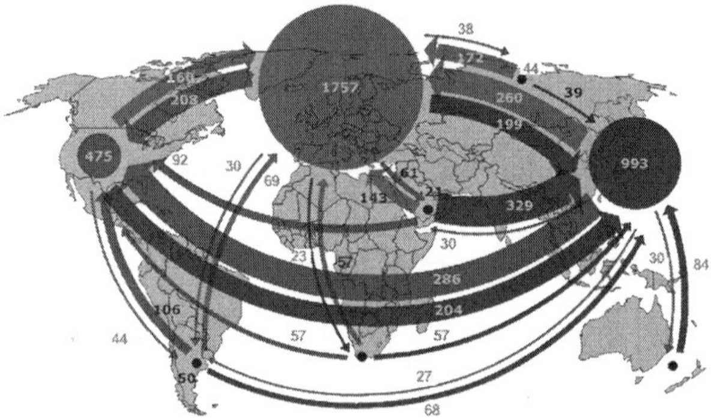

Each billion dollar flow represents millions of items; each of which require specification, are key to business efficiency, can fail in several different ways, and has the potential to develop still further. And, what is more, the volumes are doubling every five years. The figures shown on the chart are for 2006, so to calculate the figures for 2011 you would need to multiply by two. And as inter-national intermediate trade grows, so does the level of problems and issues that are at a distance from our desks, and we only have two ways to deal with these issues: either physically in person; or remotely via technology.

The result of these changes means that many people are spending more of their lives attending meetings away from their office: on airplanes, in cars, waiting at airports, or staying in hotels. In 2007, over £14.7bn was spent in business travel expenses in the UK alone;[1] the figure for the world as a whole is estimated to be

[1] £14.7bn is only for journeys involving one or more nights away from home, not including trips within a day. Source: 'Business Travel Market', Keynote 2008.

closer to \$650bn. Each respondent to our survey spent (on average) 890 hours of their time, 34 tonnes of carbon, and £19,500 in direct costs each year in business travel.[1]

Furthermore, because people are working less and less at their offices, either because they are travelling or because they are part of the trend toward office downsizing and increased home-working, even if the issues or opportunities they need to deal with *are* at their office, the chances are that they may still be dealing with them 'at a distance'.

The rise of technology

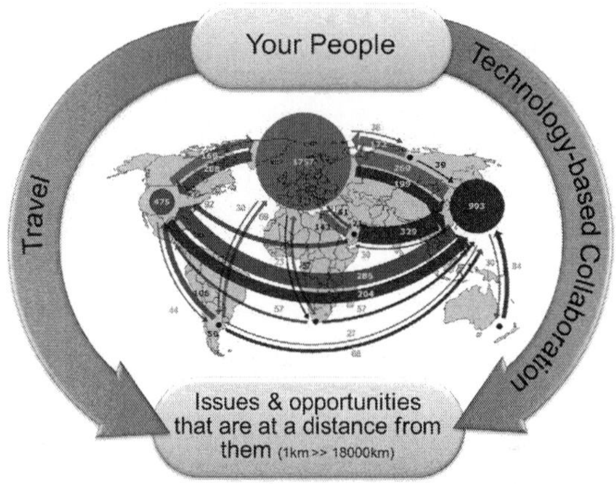

But there is a finite capacity for travel, and there is increasing pressure on travel budgets and the ecological implications of transport. As a result, technological alternatives to travel (usually referred to as virtual meetings) are becoming more and more prevalent. Some of these are developments of relatively conventional approaches such as telephone or video conferencing, but others, such as web-based meetings, are using a combination of the Internet and the capabilities of our own computers (or sometimes even smart-phones) to provide a range of enhanced features in how we work with people across geographies. These use the increasing band-width available through the Internet to provide video imaging through webcams,

[1] Survey data – see Appendix 2, reference point R.

and telephone quality audio through 'Voice over IP', and they use the resources of our own computers to share documents and collaborate on graphics. Furthermore, they are pursuing an 'always connected' picture of the future, where contacting someone three continents away is as effortless and casual as bumping into a colleague in the corridor.

Technology is changing the face of collaboration in other ways too: share points, drop boxes, and cloud computing makes working together on documents a relatively easy task.

- Scrapbook programmes capture (and share if you wish) myriad pieces of data. And intelligent web-based apps sift through masses of information to identify links and themes
- Forums and social networking sites keep conversations alive over stretches, not only of distance, but of time
- Intelligent web-based applications enable you to monitor events and programme responses from a whole range of networking options.

The technological options continue, almost daily, to grow, develop, connect-up, and become increasingly useful. Whereas the last few decades saw an explosion in the amount and availability of information, the next few are seeing an explosion in the resources to handle it effectively. You may see this as either scary or exciting, but only one of these two options will properly equip you to make best use of the immense collaborative potential that is growing all around you.

The primacy of creativity and resourcefulness

The effect of the globalisation of work and the explosion of information is a huge threat to the inherent viability of western organisations. The changes cited earlier in this chapter make commodities out of labour and expertise, and our high standard of living means that we will struggle to compete economically in either 'playing field' if they continue their trajectory to becoming 'level'.

But a heritage of teamwork, education, independent thinking, and ideas still has a value in terms of the creativity and resourcefulness we can bring to bear, both individually and collectively, providing our mechanisms of collaboration inspire and support it.

And this then is the other key development that will influence collaboration in the West – we will inevitably be part of a structure of meetings which draw the very best out of people in both the small things and the big things, and which enables those things to combine and synthesise into world-beating solutions. The inevitability of this is almost Darwinian in nature; since the West will be unable to economically sustain organisations that fail to evolve in this way – we will either be part of an organisation that evolves, or we will have to join one. Our core competitive strength lies no longer in our achievements per se, but in our rate of achievement. In the new world of global collaboration, any advance we make will soon be overtaken by the inexorable rise of information and labour, and so the only way we can stay ahead will be to travel fast.

As a result, we will either see our meetings migrate from entrenched positions to creative tension, from instruct to inspire, from policies to possibilities, from procedures to patterns, and from rhetoric to a rainbow of inputs – or we will die.

And this has big implications for our understanding of leadership. For too long our model of an effective leader was one who could communicate a compelling message, but we lost sight of the fact that the key requirement for leadership was followers, and the emphasis is not on *our* transmission but on *their* reception.

And so, while it used to be acceptable for a meeting to be primarily show and tell, with a predominance of presentation, and debates which centre around the more vociferous team members, and for others in the meeting to remain silent (i.e. the mechanisms of 'transmission' in leadership) we will no longer be able to afford these inefficiencies. Let's face it, if the work we are instructing them to do requires no creative or experience-based input from our people then it could be done just as easily, and far more cheaply, in a low-cost country. We cannot afford not to engage (and develop) the best that our people have to offer, and to access that on a continual basis. And this means that our meetings will need to better access the potential outlined in Chapter 1; they will need to 'draw out' rather than 'drive in', they will need to encourage participation, ideas, and insights from all the team (especially the more reflective ones) and to build commitment and confidence through this; in other words, they will have to focus on the 'reception' elements of leadership.

This difference between a transmission focus and a reception focus for leadership has fundamental implications for how we understand and interpret the aims of a meeting as illustrated by the diagram below.[1] How we see what we are trying to achieve will very much depend on how we see our leadership role (transmission on the left and reception on the right) and while the left-hand side of the diagram is reasonably well supported by the techniques of presentation and debate, the right hand side is not.

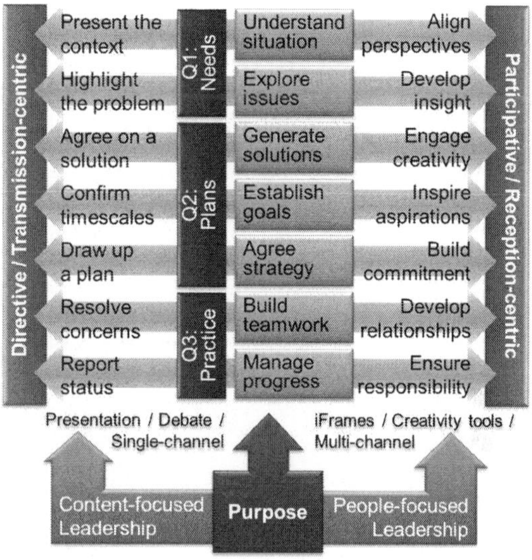

This does not in any way preclude presentations as a start point, but we will need to see far more participative techniques used to enable our people to assimilate, engage with, and then further develop our initial ideas. How else can we 'engage the practical creativity and resourcefulness of our people in bringing about a step change in performance'? And, as the future unfolds, we in the West are going to need a whole staircase of step changes.

The need to differentiate between meetings

As we engage more of our people's creativity and insight, the nature of our meetings will change in other ways too. Some of that creativity and insight may well be submitted directly into the meeting, but far more of it will emerge through sparking-off colleagues, in refinement through dialogue, and through incubation

[1] Please refer back to the sidebar on page 37

of trains of thought initiated by the meeting. All of these things require full engagement of people in the initial meeting, but they also need this to be supplemented by other, more fragmented, interactions – what we used to call corridor conversations (except that the corridor is now somewhat longer than it used to be). But here, the technology developments mentioned earlier come to our aid, and we can see this in the promotional videos of web-meeting providers, who tend to portray a vision of bright young things seamlessly making contact with others at a moment's notice, obtaining an open and engaged response, opening up the contact to include one or two more smiling, intelligent, and engaged individuals, who are clearly at one with what is to be achieved, and who inevitably provide the knowledge and insight they need to progress their project to the next stage.

It is a very attractive picture of the future, one has to admit, but is this the future we should be preparing for? If so, there are two very important questions that arise: 1. Where have all the slightly more awkward or misaligned people that you and I tend to encounter in *our* meetings gone? 2. What has happened prior to this vision to magically address the issues of Chapter 2?

To begin to answer these questions we need to take a slight detour to the work of Jean Piaget, reported by Arie de Geus in his book *The Living Company*, and the idea that there are two different types of learning: learning by assimilation and learning by accommodation.

Learning by assimilation is relatively easy learning, it is about gathering knowledge which fits easily into our existing structures for how the world works and our place within it. This sort of learning fills out the gaps in an existing picture and hangs on ready-made hooks within current frameworks of understanding – the new information sits easily alongside old information and does not distort the overall picture. An example of learning by assimilation is to accept that the blue colour in our cherished corporate image which we have been working on for months is Pantone 18-3943, and is called Iris.

Learning by accommodation however is a more uncomfortable form of learning, it involves accepting that the framework on which we have been hanging our knowledge is flawed in some way and needs to be changed; it requires an internal structural change in our beliefs, ideas and/or attitudes. It is difficult because although changing our models of thinking and belief to something which more closely represents reality does move us forward, it actually feels like taking a number of steps backward. An example of learning by accommodation is to discover that our cherished corporate image, which we have been working on for months, is actually disliked by most of our team.

In this sense, all meetings are about learning in one form or the other. In some meetings, where we are clearly all on the same page, following the same script toward a commonly agreed end-point, our learning is going to be a straightforward sharing of key pieces of information and opinion that move us all forward in our intended direction – learning by assimilation. In other meetings, where there is confusion about the situation and the best way to handle it, or where there may be conflicting beliefs and attitudes held by those who need to reach agreement, there is clearly some level of accommodation that is required by at least some of the parties present – each of whom currently believe their 'framework' to be the correct one.

The first of these two meetings is the type that is commonly portrayed in promotions of web-based meetings – where the 'play' is clear and the 'actors' are aligned in their delivery of it. See the lower left quadrant of the diagram above. We call these *Tag Meetings* because they are about a simple handover of information, and to reflect the idea of hanging those *Tags* on the hooks in a shared, valid, framework of understanding. You can probably reflect on some of your own meetings that have gone this way – they are usually simple, brief, to the point, and a delight to be part of.

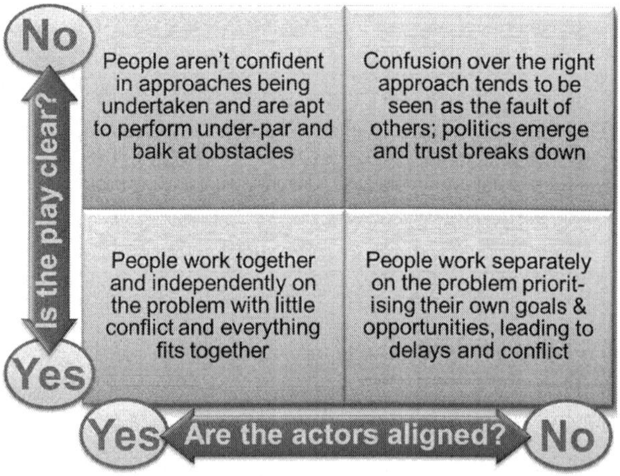

But effective Tag Meetings are dependent on the 'play being clear' and the 'actors aligned', and the question has to be asked: 'How did they become that way?' Added to which, even though the play may be 'clear' to begin with, time and unexpected developments gradually erode the consensus and alignment that has been achieved, and undermine the assumptions that lie behind the chosen direction. At these points, a simple presentation and exchange of views is often insufficient to bring the insight and shared commitment that is necessary to make efficient progress, and a greater level of engagement, creativity and process becomes necessary to reconcile the emerging divisions.

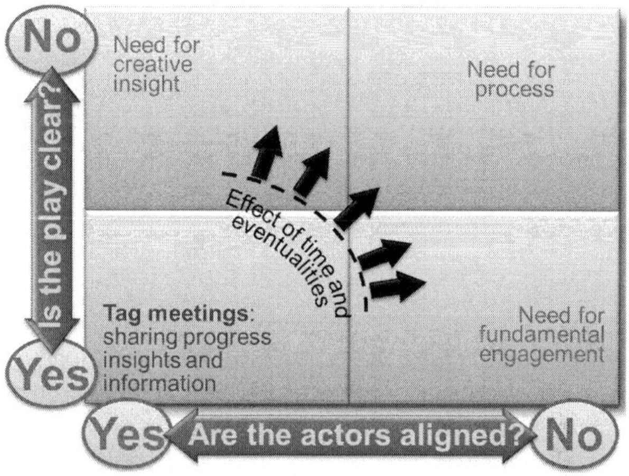

This then brings us on to the second type of meeting. We call these *Tackle Meetings* because people have to wrestle with their own under-standing of the situation, and with other people's, to reach a common framework which has the necessary commitment and support to ensure progress going forward. You probably have some experience of these meetings as well – they either took a degree of pain and trouble to reach a conclusion, or they ended with a series of actions but no real confidence in the commitment to deliver those actions, or sometimes both. Simple presentations and discussions have their place in these meetings but are rarely sufficient to bring about the 'learning by accommodation' that is needed. More sophisticated tools are advised in order to inspire the creative insight, and handle the variety of participation required for people to change their models and bring their commitment behind a common way forward. Frustration arises when we try to bring about the 'learning by accommodation' necessary in these meetings, armed only with tools that are suited to 'learning by assimilation' – but sadly this is often the case.

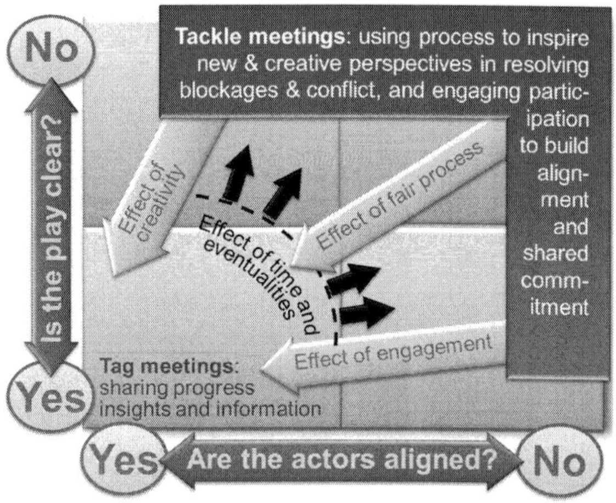

The bad news is that Tackle Meetings need a degree of planning and forethought if they are to efficiently bring people together into an effective strategy (direction/plan) and inspire a level of alignment and commitment sufficient to ensure rapid progress. The better news is that if Tackle Meetings are well designed, they are not needed anywhere near as frequently as Tag Meetings. One well-run Tackle Meeting is often enough to support several weeks' (or even months') worth of Tag Meetings. The good news is that the time invested in planning a good Tackle Meeting is a fraction of the time you will end up wasting without one.

Understanding Tag Meetings

But let us start with Tag Meetings. Tag Meetings happen naturally over the telephone, through emails, via web-cams and conference calls. Tag Meetings, in the context of an appropriately aligned and directed environment are easy, and they are not the events that cause us to travel half-way around the globe (or even 50 miles up the road). They are also not the types of event that cause the issues in performance reported in Chapter 2 – those statistics are caused by attempting to hold Tag type meetings in a context of unclear direction and misaligned participants – those statistics are caused by holding Tag Meetings when Tackle Meetings are required.

Tag Meetings are primarily about a flow of information from those who have it to those who need it. Sometimes this information is clear and straightforward, and sometimes it needs to be worked upon by interaction. Sometimes the exchange involves only two members of the team, sometimes a subset, and sometimes all of the team.

But the question needs to be asked, do Tag Meetings require a traditional meeting at all, or are there other mechanisms that will work more effectively and economically? For instance, if we look back at the diagram introduced on page 70 and reproduced here, could we do more through forums, or share points etc., or by exploring other elements of synchronous or asynchronous interaction.

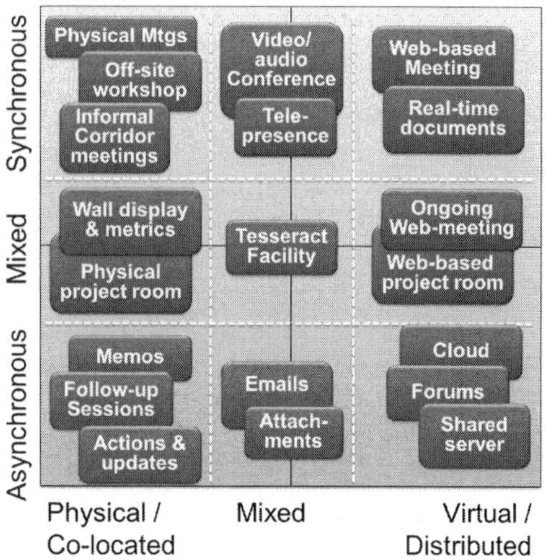

Physical Tag Meetings are often inefficient because not everybody needs to be involved all of the time, and Tag information is often better exchanged on an as-needed basis rather than according to a weekly schedule – hence the 'Always Connected' vision.

There is, however, one sharing of information that does benefit from a physical (or at least synchronous) meeting, and that is the confirmation that we are all aligned and all working together; in other words that we can be confident that we are still firmly ensconced in the lower left-hand quadrant of the diagram on page 80. The need for this sort of meeting should not be underestimated, and it does a lot to maintain morale and raise energy (providing of course you really *are* in the lower left quadrant) and it can be done quite quickly and as part of sharing other information which really does involve the whole team e.g., overall progress or external developments.

Meetings which are primarily centred around a presentation are typically Tag Meetings. They assume that the information they are conveying will be instantly assimilated into the thinking of their audience, and they typically assume that non participation is 'assent'. Sometimes they will ask if everyone is in agreement but, as we showed on page 40, there are a range of levels of commitment and such meetings can be useful where the base level of commitment is high, but they will not raise it significantly where the base level is low. For this, organisations will require some learning by accommodation through a Tackle Meeting.

Understanding Tackle Meetings

The ideal place for a team to function is in the lower left-hand quadrant of the diagram, but it is rare for a team to start there. And even when they are in this place, there is usually a flow of developments which will draw the team out into the other quadrants. This is entirely natural, and in a complex world almost inevitable, especially as we begin to function in areas of greater uncertainty and we try to access more of our people's creativity, resourcefulness and character.

However, the mechanisms required to draw people back into clarity and alignment depend in large part on which quadrant the team has drifted into; on whether developments have muddied the play, or divided the actors, or both. And the type of Tackle Meeting managers use can fall into three camps, as shown in the diagram on the right, and in the explanations below:

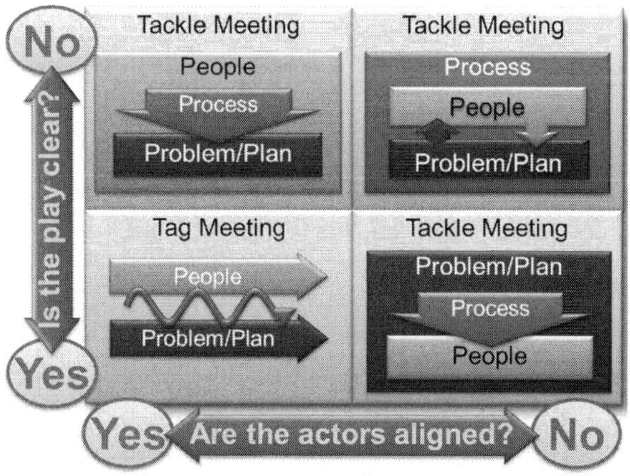

- **Play unclear/actors misaligned** – It is this situation which managers are most likely to encounter at the start of a project or piece of work. Here the Tackle Meeting tends to be formative in nature, enabling people to work on the problem in a structured way, while gaining insights into their own responsibilities and relationships within that. It is about breaking down the problem and moving through its definition and planned resolution step by step, and at each step consciously considering how the roles and relationships of the team are unfolding. The key to success here is to ensure that the problem or intention is first defined at a level which engages with a shared goal for the group (even at the highest level – the success of the organisation – if no shared goal can be found at more detailed levels). It is then broken down objectively through tangible evidence and avoiding divisive opinion and blame, until practical steps become clear, and people are appointed to them. It is very much about getting the problem to work on the people while the people work on the problem.

- **Play unclear/actors aligned** – This situation occurs when either a well-established team is given a new problem, or where the problem itself shifts. It is very common in projects which move through stages of resolution, and where the issues need to be tackled at an increasingly detailed level – for instance when they move from identifying a solution to planning its implementation. Key to making progress in this quadrant is opening up the problem through insight and creativity, to ensure that it embraces all of the possibilities, before focusing back down on a way forward.
- **Play clear/actors misaligned** – Sadly, the most common cause of drifting into this quadrant is organisational politics; where vested interests shift or seek to exploit emerging advantages. It is often referred to as 'hidden agendas', and needs to be addressed early and firmly to avoid generating waste and inefficiency. Key to progress in this quadrant is returning to the problem which all the actors have been assembled to tackle, and then working through the steps to identify the beginnings of disagreement. This enables the group to begin asking how they need to widen their understanding of the problem in order to provide a valid platform for including the hidden agenda. Bringing the agenda into the light in this way, and giving it validity, actually refines away the subversive baggage that may have become attached to it and, in doing so, has made it a common issue for the whole team.

Tackle Meetings can meet all three of these needs, but they do it best through creative use of participative tools rather than verbal debate. Paradoxically, in Tackle Meetings, the boardroom table is often an impediment to process, as it is a symbolic reinforcement of division and 'sides'.

Understanding Compound Meetings

From the foregoing, we can see that Tag and Tackle Meetings are totally different from each other both in terms of their purpose and in terms of their ideal form. For this reason, they are best kept separate from each other.

However, sometimes it is convenient and economical to have both Tag and Tackle elements as part of one meeting. Where this is the case, the following two issues are the most likely to undermine that economy:

- Failing to be explicit within the meeting about exactly what is going to happen and why, and failing to select the most appropriate and efficient approach for the different elements.
- Throwing in other items simply because the group is 'having a meeting', instead of evaluating each item on its merits, and excluding those that can either be done in better ways or which may detract from what it actually trying to be achieved in the meeting.

However, if the meeting is mindful of these issues, and is clear about the purpose of each item, there are no fundamental reasons why compound meetings should not be successful.

In summary

The requirement for people to engage with issues and opportunities at a distance is now a major part of most managers' time and is increasing rapidly. Fortunately, corresponding advances in technology means that more of these issues and opportunities can be handled without the need for travel,

However, competition from cheaper and more focused sources of supply reaches us through these channels, and is driving us to focus on and exploit our own strengths.

All of these factors will fundamentally change the way we conduct meetings in the future.

Insight: Questions for reflection

To what extent can you identify work in your own organisation involving more issues and opportunities 'at a distance'?

How familiar are you with the range of collaboration techniques that currently exist, and how likely is it that they might now have something to offer you?

To what extent do your meetings 'engage the practical creativity and resourcefulness of your people'? Is the answer different when you consider the meetings you attend as opposed to those you run, and is it all the people or just some of them?

Chapter 4

What Can We Learn From Success?

In short

Some meetings are successful because they have to be, and we can learn a lot from these in improving how our own meetings are managed.

The key problem with traditional meetings, those that are still rooted in an approach which goes back centuries, is that they tend to take place at the level of the content of the meeting – everybody, including the person who is leading the meeting, has their mind on 'what' is being decided, and virtually nobody has a thought for 'how' it is being decided, or 'how best' to decide it. As a result, nobody really has an objective view of the efficiency of the meeting in achieving its ends, apart from perhaps a slight sense of frustration and an occasional thought that there must be a better way to do this.

There is however, one particular type of meeting for which this is not true. It is a meeting that is becoming increasingly prevalent, but usually only on a once or twice a year basis for many people. It is a meeting which is almost always successful in influencing the performance of the organisation and in generating commitment to deliver its conclusions, but it is expensive, and so it tends to be reserved for the most important strategy setting/aligning work in the organisation. The meeting to which we are referring is the off-site (often externally-facilitated) workshop.

Sadly, workshops in their current form are too costly to run[1] for every type of decision that the organisation needs to make but they do contain some very important clues as to what makes a meeting successful:

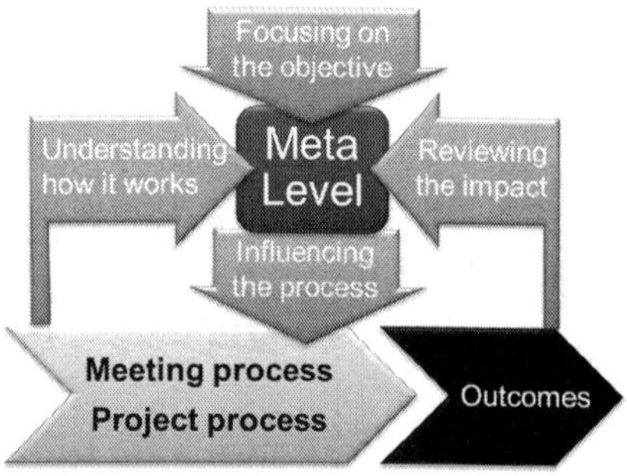

- They are designed at the 'meta' level; a level which can see the overall context and the patterns within that, and can determine 'how' to deliver the best (supported) decision
- They are targeted at an accurate perception of the current situation, based on researching the objectives and the gap
- They utilise a multi-channel approach to ensure that everybody's perspectives and ideas are included and that the conclusion is arrived at through logic rather than dominance
- They use a process which includes a wide range of techniques and tools to engage people's interest and draw out their creativity and their commitment
- They 'facilitate' that process to its successful conclusion; monitoring the 'how' and realigning it where needs be
- They have a reputation for delivering results which encourages participants to 'step up their game'.

[1] Average charge levied by Tesseract Management Systems for preparing and facilitating a 10–20 person workshop in 2010 was £20k.

But there are a number of issues concerning them as well.

In this chapter we will begin to unpack these points to take a better look at them, and to see what we can draw from considering the first practical revolution in meeting design for over 2,000 years.

Grasping the 'meta'

There is a big responsibility attached to receiving a five or six figure sum for designing and facilitating an off-site workshop. The sums of money involved carry a certain professional expectation for assured success, and that is before you realise that the subject of the workshop carries the responsibility of maintaining hundreds, if not thousands, of people's continued financial security. It is not a responsibility to take on lightly.

While there are many detractors of management consultancy, and while there are people within its ranks that really should not be there, it is at its heart a profession, and in the main it takes a professional approach to fulfilling its responsibilities, particularly when they are (and they usually are) high profile and well remunerated. As with other professional disciplines, such as medicine and engineering, they simply cannot afford to leave things to chance, and so their success is rooted in a methodology which:

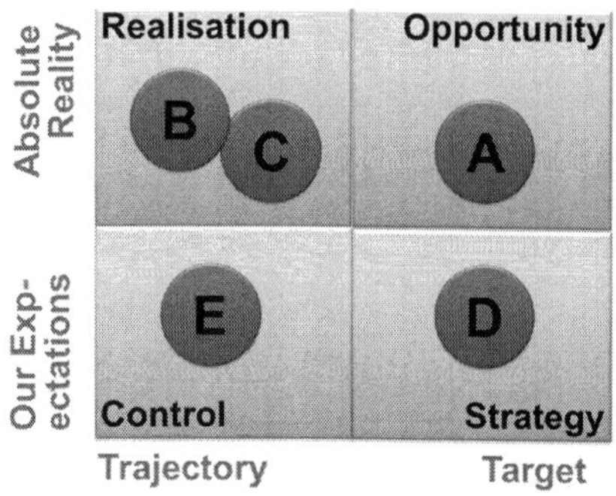

A. Determines clear, value-based, client-verified, standards of success
B. Researches the salient features of the current situation and analyses the critical factors for achieving that success
C. Selects, from a wide range of available best practice, those which can be most appropriately combined to deliver success
D. Pulls these into a comprehensive and robust strategy
E. Carefully and objectively monitors the strategy while it is being delivered, and makes adjustments to ensure success.

Looking back over this list you can see that these professional perspectives are all taken from a level that looks down on the situation and understands the context, the flow, and the interactions.[1] For the doctor and the engineer, these perspectives are fairly obvious: a doctor does not immediately climb inside a body to make the blood flow; nor the engineer leap into a turbo-charged V12.[2] Professionalism is all about working at the logical level which systematically determines the required outcomes in the level below. It is about taking our thinking to a level above the level of activities, results, and details. We call this level the meta-level.[3]

---

[1] Compare with the list of points (and their plot shown in the diagram in the top right corner of this page) with the diagram on page 37, Chapter 1.
[2] Although the author has been tempted on occasion.
[3] Etymology: From Ancient Greek μετά (meta).
1. Transcending, encompassing, 2. Pertaining to a level above or beyond.

Sadly, unlike his or her professional colleagues in other disciplines, the professional manager often finds themselves focusing on specific details and outcomes rather than the overall patterns of performance and the processes which influence them.[1] It is true that doctors and engineers do this also from time to time, but those who do so regularly are apt to find themselves in court on charges of professional negligence – an appropriate term which accurately reflects neglect of the professional perspective, neglect of the meta-level. It is also a concept which is just beginning to make its presence felt in the world of management, particularly where accidents have arisen as a result of systematic failures.[2]

Are successful consultants then just managers who have grasped the concept of the meta-level? There are a number of reasons why there may be a grain of truth in this. Certainly their role means that they do not have a valid option to consider themselves as an integral part of a solution, and a lack of familiarity with the specifics forces them to consider alternatives to engaging with the detail. But probably the biggest factor in consultants grasping the meta-level is something infinitely more visceral.

There is frankly nothing quite as uncomfortable for a management consultant as a workshop which is starting on a headlong plummet to going 'wrong'. Most of those who have experienced such unpleasantness will do anything in their power to prevent it happening again. And those who don't tend to be filtered out of the gene pool by natural selection (going hungry from a lack of references and a lack of work).

---

[1] Chapter 4, *Managing by Design*, Clargo, Tesseracts, 2002.
[2] Financial Times, 23 April 2009, re Peter Eaton, Cotswold Geotechnical.

Off-site workshops are successful because they have to be successful. You pay a professional fee, and you get a professional approach. But there is no fundamental reason why professional managers should not access the meta-level for the design and facilitation of their own meetings. It is more difficult for someone immersed in the detail and under a lot of time pressure to pull themselves up to the meta-level, but perhaps the biggest issue for many, is simply failing to remember that the meta-level is there at all.

Researching the objectives/gap

So, what do people do when they get to the meta-level? The first thing management consultants (professional facilitators) do when they access the meta-level is to take a good look around. Before they try to influence or control the patterns, they need to see what the patterns are – that sounds a bit abstract, so let us narrow it down a bit with the story of a simple game which provides a lot of insight.

There is an exercise called 'The Rope Square' which involves four members of a blindfolded team positioning themselves at the corners of the biggest perfect square they can achieve in ten minutes. To assist them they have a 20m length of rope (which they cannot touch until the start of the exercise, after they have been blindfolded) and 15 minutes' preparation time during which they are sighted and can plan out their strategy.

At the end of the exercise they take off their blindfolds, evaluate their square, and have the model solution explained to them (if they did not arrive at it themselves). They then have 15 minutes to list all the things about their approach and their behaviours which helped their progress and achievement, and all the things that hindered it, and these are documented by the facilitator on a flipchart. An example is shown on the right.

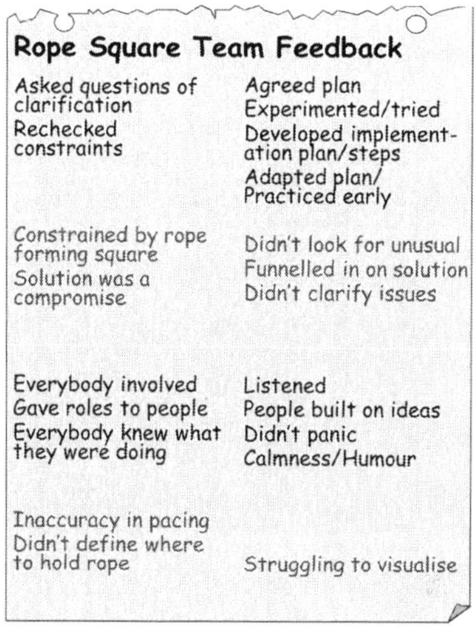

Initially, as the facilitator writes things down, the group are intrigued by the pattern of where the facilitator writes them; different points seem to be written in different quadrants of the flipchart – positives in green, negatives in red. When they have finished, the facilitator asks them to describe the general theme of the things that have been written in each of the four quadrants. In doing so, the facilitator asks them to join him or her at the meta-level, and take a look at the patterns which determined success.

The themes are always the same: understanding of goals, effectiveness of process, clarity of roles, and quality of interpersonal interaction. No matter who does the exercise, the same four themes emerge in the feedback, sometimes with more red than green, sometimes vice versa, but always the same four themes. And, as the facilitator draws out the themes, the team begins to realise, aside from any theory or rhetoric, that in a very real and practical sense they were successful to the extent that those themes were picked out in green and unsuccessful to the extent that they were picked out in red.[1]

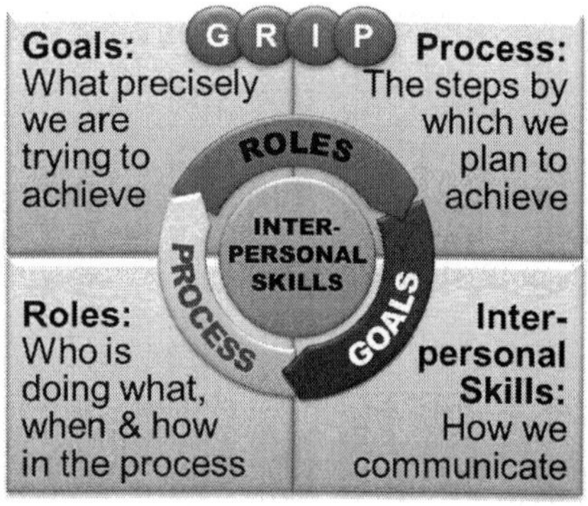

And it does not matter whether the team are laying out a rope square, planning a new product, fixing a problem, delivering to a deadline or running an entire organisation: To the extent that the objectives are clear, that they have a good process, that everybody knows what they are doing within it, and that they communicate well to resolve issues, they are successful. And to the extent that the converse of these things are true, they are destined to failure.

At one level, this may sound obvious, and yet despite our acceptance of the importance of these four factors, they are rarely treated with the care and attention that is commensurate with that importance, and in very many cases they have drifted off-track and are causing issues for the efficiency and effectiveness of what is taking place.

For this reason, it is very common to find that consultants engaged in designing and supporting an off-site workshop will be conducting interviews with a number of the key staff from the very outset of their assignment, and the focus of these interviews will pertain to objectives, process, roles, and communication.

[1] Dr Bill Pigg, R&D Director at Systagenix Wound Management, utilises these terms (Goals, Roles, Interpersonal skills and Process) as a useful acronym GRIP, and an apposite phrase: Get a GRIP on meetings.

The point is, that professional facilitators take a look around at the meta-level and, when they do, it is basically those four things (objectives, process, roles, and communication) that they are looking for. Professional facilitators look for them because their success (that the meeting they will facilitate has a positive impact on the organisation) will be dependent on the extent to which those four things are present and working well, and so they need to know how well they are working at the moment, and what they need to do about them in the meeting.

There are a number of ways they can do this, but one of the best is simply to talk to people and ask them questions about their view of how the group fares in terms of:

- Their perception on what they are trying to achieve, and how consistent that is with other people's perceptions
- Their confidence and concerns about the approach currently being taken to deliver the goals of the group
- How they see their role within that approach, and how confident and committed they are to delivering that role
- How well their role works in relation to other people's roles, and the quality of teamwork that takes place between them

Is the *Play* clear?

Are the *Actors* aligned?

You can see, from the linkage to the grey boxes on the right (Is the play clear? Are the actors aligned?), the resonance this has with the issues that require Tackle Meetings.[1]

[1] See page 80.

It takes a bit of time to work through these things, but given that success is founded on these four pillars, there is nothing more important at the meta-level than getting them right.[1] Whether the topic of the meeting is problem solving, performance review, planning, or innovation, and whether the level of the meeting is corporate, departmental, team, or workgroup, the performance the meeting delivers depends on the quality of these four pillars.

The concept of a multi-channel approach

Off-site meetings would get fairly boring if they were simply a series of presentations and questions from the floor, and the people who organise them are aware that such passive participation is not particularly good at changing people's attitudes and developing common commitment,[2] and therefore passive participation is not particularly good at bringing about change.

Breakout groups provide a good way of getting greater levels of participation, but they are still essentially single-channel in nature, and are vulnerable to being dominated by a few strong wills while the more reflective members let it all happen around them.

[1] Reference back to page 96; 'they were successful to the extent that those themes were picked out in green, and unsuccessful to the extent that they were picked out in red'.
[2] *Building a Company of Citizens*, Manville and Ober, HBR, January 2003.

But if the organisers of off-site meetings are to be truly successful in bringing everybody behind a common conclusion, with full commitment to push it through, they know that they have to utilise some practical psychology in the design of their meetings.

Individual and group commitment to a decision grows when the people involved:

- Understand the reasons why the decision has to be made, and the benefits of it being made now
- Have had a chance to see any concerns they have included within the decision making process and properly addressed
- Believe that the decision was arrived at after consideration of a range of possible options, including their own ideas
- Recognise that, at a pragmatic level, there is not some better option that has been disregarded or overlooked
- Feel that the process for selecting the chosen option was objective and fair in reflecting different viewpoints, including their own
- Have not allowed their ego to become attached to an option that has been rejected.

The process of achieving this is reflected in the diagram on the right. Good decisions, which carry people with them, are made by:

- Opening up: considering all the options, including those from outside

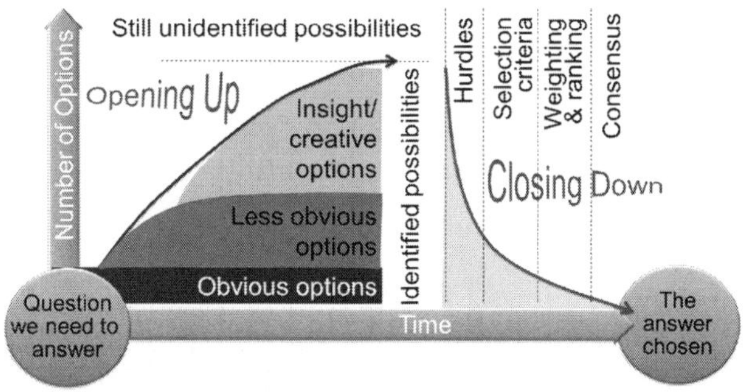

the group, and drawing out creative inputs from the group members themselves

- Closing down: reaching a rational conclusion through appropriate criteria in a clear and transparent manner.

The irony of single-channel meeting approaches is that group participation is most useful in the opening up stage, where the interaction of different minds generate new insights and possibilities, but the structure of single-channel meetings lends itself best to closing down where one person leads a methodical selection with relevant and sequential input from others.

But what is the practical alternative to this single-channel approach?

In the 1980s, the Japanese led the world in the quality of their management approaches. Having been defeated in World War II, they sought to understand the strengths of their 'adversary' and in the fifties and sixties enthusiastically embraced the messages of people like Deming and Juran on the topic of quality – a concept which resonates with Japanese traditions of craftsmanship.

Over the years, the Japanese adapted these approaches to better reflect their characteristics of consensus, and of avoiding the more exuberant aspects of arguing for an outcome, and out of this evolved what became known as Total Quality Management.[1]

About this time, the Japanese Union of Scientists and Engineers (a more powerful and influential body that their name would imply in the West) began to research the best decision making practices adopted by Japanese companies, and arrived at what they called

---

[1] *Managing Quality*, Garvin, Macmillan, 1988.

'The Seven Quality Tools' and 'The Seven Management and Planning Tools'.[1] The interesting thing about these tools is that they each lend themselves to multi-channel input: they are large and can be worked upon using a wall or flipchart, they are simple and visual and everybody can understand what is going on, and they are open and solicit engagement across the group. And, perhaps most importantly of all, they provide an excellent basis for meeting the psychological needs for commitment to a decision that were bulleted on page 99.

In fact, for those responsible for ensuring that an off-site event is successful in engaging commitment from the organisation, they are a God-send, and so it is of little surprise that we are beginning to find them (and their derivatives) increasingly designed into the structure of such workshops. Some common examples of these tools are shown in the panel on the next page.

Although these examples of a multi-channel approach tend to reflect the mechanisms of a Tackle Meeting, all that you have read so far has lessons for Tag Meetings as well.

It is also beneficial to consider the process of Tag Meetings from a meta perspective; understanding the quality of alignment around objectives, process, roles, and communication is key to confirming that a Tag Meeting is appropriate.

[1] *The Memory Jogger Plus+*, Brassard, Goal QPC, 1989.

Common examples of multi-channel tools

- Affinity diagrams – for drawing out people's ideas on a topic and then grouping them so that they can be prioritised

- Ishikawa diagrams – for exploring the relationship between cause and effect and the implications of a chosen solution

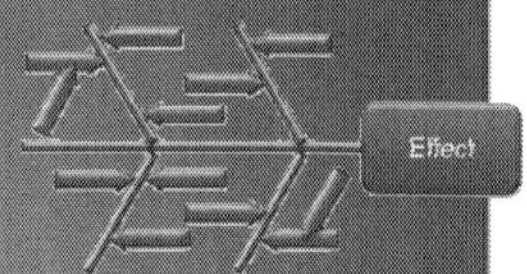

- Interrelationship diagrams – for exploring the links and causality between events and other relevant entities

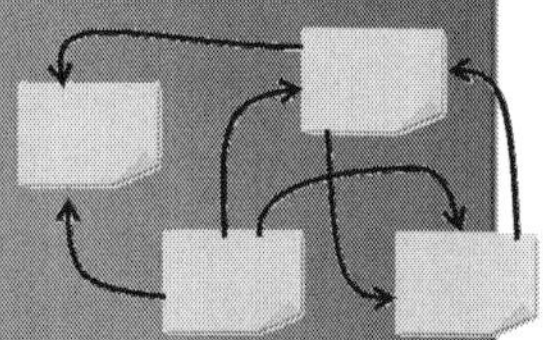

- Tree diagrams – for breaking down situations into their relevant components while keeping an overview of the whole

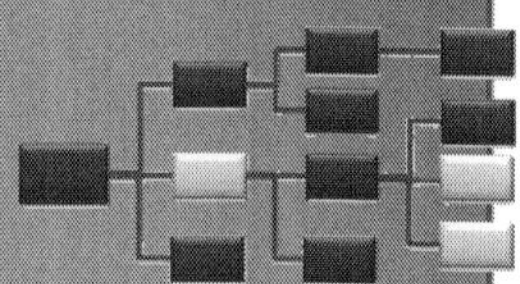

- Matrix diagrams – for exploring influence and impact, particularly on defined criteria, and thereby selection and prioritisation

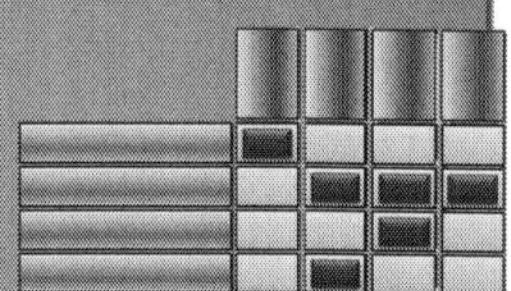

- Force-field diagram – for looking at the balancing forces on a situation, particularly in respect of motives.

These are explained in greater detail in Appendix 4.

But even more importantly, if we are willing to stretch our horizons on the potential of virtual meetings and asynchronous working, then we can grasp the concept of a multi-channel process for Tag Meetings as well – via mechanisms such as the cloud, permanent web-based meeting rooms, share points, forums etc.

Designing the process

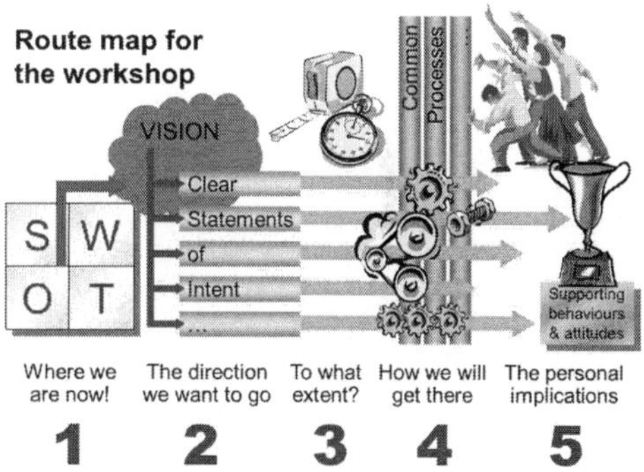

In a very real sense, the success of an off-site workshop is not taken out of the room on the numerous rolls of flipcharts taken from the walls, or in the notes recorded for typing and distribution, but in what has changed in the heads of the people who took part in it; the change in their beliefs, their resolve, their relationships with each other and their relationship with the conclusions of the workshop. But is that not true in principle of all meetings?

Therefore, the process of the workshop is only successful to the extent that it engages with and influences people's thoughts and emotions. For the workshop to be successful, the participants have to have been taken on a journey where they can see the right thing to do and then commit to it. Workshops are first and foremost a place of individual and organisational learning (as are all meetings,[1] but sadly people often fail to recognise that fact).

[1] Please refer back to page 78

There is a danger here that you might read the last paragraph and think it smacks of manipulation, but that is far, far away from what is intended here. Harold Evans, a famous editor of *The Sunday Times*, described manipulation as 'forcing someone to make a decision while withholding some of the facts', and the approach we are advocating is quite the reverse. We are merely reflecting that any new understanding which leads to a change in behaviour is 'learning' (whether it arises as the result of intervention from a 'teacher' or not), and that it can be very helpful to consider it as such, primarily for the insight that this now gives us in practical ways to bring it about.

Two of those insights concern an educationalist called David Kolb, whose observations[1] lead to the concepts of a 'Learning Cycle' (that we all need to work through a cycle of steps to arrive at learning and to sustainably install it in our thinking) and 'Learning Styles' (that we all have different preferences for stages within that cycle).

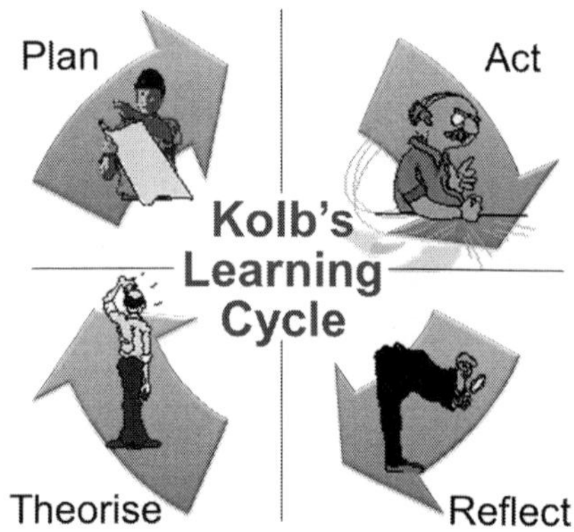

These principles are evident in all good workshop design:

- They encourage rational explanations and logical arguments for people to understand the reasoning
- They provide opportunities for people to test out their own thinking and handle the responses that emerge

[1] 'Toward an applied theory of experiential learning', Kolb and Fry, in *Theories of Group Process*, Cooper (ed.), John Wiley, 1975.

- They give time for people to reflect on what they have seen emerge, and to reconcile this with their thinking
- They encourage people to plan their next steps.

Through a balance of explanation and involvement, of single- and multi-channel engagement, good workshop designers structure a process which combines these various approaches to provide a learning environment which honours the learning cycle, and provides a balance of opportunity for the different learning styles.

But this is rarely achieved by accident. The following diagram shows a small section of an off-site workshop plan which reflects the structured thinking about each part of the workshop: What it is intended to achieve (objective), how it takes place (process), what it requires to allow it to happen (inputs), its timings, and what happens to the outputs.

Time	Item	Durn.	Objective	Inputs	Process	Outputs
08.10	**Process Content**	30 mins	To explore what each process contains and what it does not	Process flipcharts Slide explaining approach	Put up flipcharts headed with the various process titles and then split the group into teams to think through what each process includes within it (the key sub-processes and activities) and populate these using post-it notes. Give them a few minutes to walk round and add to the others.	
08.40	**Process Clarification**	40 mins	To provide an opportunity for the group to further define the processes in terms of their contents and boundaries	Process Discussion Proformas Slide on how it works	Organise the tables for a 'roof' discussion, and explain the process people will go through to clarify any overlaps and boundaries between their various processes Explain the process, and give people 8 minutes to clarify each boundary, and move post-its accordingly	Refined sheets of what each process links includes
09.20	**Grid of processes against objectives**	40 mins	To clarify exactly what each process can contribute to achieving our goals	Grid of process vs objectives Criteria (example) for a good post-it note Brief	Split people up to cover one process per team. Get each team to think through what practical contributions each process can make in delivering against the top level objective and write these out clearly on post-it notes (unambiguous). Invite them to review any 'hows' from the objectives exercise for ideas, and any current plans and ideas, and also to take the opportunity to think creatively and include best practice ideas – encourage them to quantify where possible	Grid of contributions

This level of planning helps the workshop designer structure a logical and effective process which engages and changes people's thinking. It also allows them to objectively challenge their own design: Does it utilise inputs and creativity? Could more be done off-line? Does it grow potential as well as performance? Does it reflect and reinforce the culture?

Because each workshop tends to be different, each session plan tends to be different, but the same is not entirely true for other meetings, and here the manager holds an advantage over the consultant.

Facilitating the outcomes

Of course, there is no such thing as a perfect process, certainly not when dealing with people. No matter how well designed the initial process may be, it will go off-track if its progress is not carefully facilitated.

Facilitators are the custodians of 'how' things are being done. They are people who maintain their awareness in the meta-level of the meeting, observing the patterns that develop, comparing these against the process that was intended, and making small adjustments and interventions to keep things on track to a successful and valuable outcome.

Key within this is maintaining the 'essentials of success'[1] at a functional level within the meeting:

- Are people clear and in agreement about what they are trying to achieve in this activity?
- Are they supportive of, and working in line with, an agreed and plausible approach to deliver that objective?
- Does everybody understand their role within that approach, and are they willing and able to effect that role?
- Is the communication that is taking place constructive, supportive, and likely to encourage progress?

[1] Explained alongside the diagram on page 95.

On this last point, the facilitator sometimes has a very special role to play in group discussions, and that is to maintain an easy flow while avoiding any sense of a free-for-all. In a free-for-all, people listen for a gap in the dialogue to get their point in as soon as they can. In a worst-case scenario this can lead to speakers being interrupted the moment they pause for breath, people talking over each other, or having side-conversations. Even in fairly minor cases, people might be listening intently for another person to finish, but they are not actually listening to what that finish is; the absence of a pause between one person finishing and the next person talking is a sure sign that the focus of the meeting has shifted from listening to speaking. Two things commonly emerge from this: People end up interjecting to get the floor without thinking through the most efficient way to get their message across, and people (rightly) feel that they were not listened to the first time, so begin to repeat their points.

If, however, the facilitator highlights this issue, agrees ground rules around brevity, listening, and not repeating points, and then uses a non-intrusive technique for 'queuing' the inputs,[1] then people find that they are much better able to concentrate on the content rather than the gaps, they feel listened to, and consensus is more easily and more quickly achieved.

In summary, good facilitators are not influenced by the content of what is emerging in the decision (that is the responsibility of others), merely the quality of the approach by which the decisions

[1] One that works very well is for the facilitator to get people to catch his/her eye if they want to speak, and then keep them in order in their head. Before they invite the next person to speak, they run through the remaining order e.g., 'Sue, and then Lucy, and then Fred', and simply drop those who have spoken off the front of their list, and add new ones to the end of it.

were delivered. This is an uncomfortable concept for many people, because they infer all sorts of incorrect value statements from it, such as 'the process is more important than the outcome'. What they overlook in these judgements is:

- The quality of the process is ultimately evaluated by the quality of the outcome
- The process *can* change (even frequently) but it is still the process
- More successful outcomes are delivered through process than through a collection of random acts
- A sequence of acts that are not random, however they arise, are still a process, and still need to be monitored to ensure they are taking the group in the right direction.

If we return again to the essentials (page 95), process is a key factor in success. Processes are good things which reflect intelligence and forethought, but which are flexible to emerging realities. The problem is that people sometimes tend to confuse 'process' and 'procedure';[1] and their experience of procedures tends to be rigid, bureaucratic and sometimes counterproductive – this is not what we mean at all.

Because 'good' meetings are a place and time of learning, for everybody involved, the emerging insights cannot be fully predicted from the outset. Therefore we see that the process sometimes needs to flex in order to best accommodate those

[1] Wikipedia defines a business process as 'a collection of related, structured activities or tasks that produce a specific service or product (serve a particular goal)' and a procedure as 'a specified series of actions or operations which have to be executed in the same manner in order to always obtain the same result'. The differences are subtle, but crucially important.

insights if it is to utilise them effectively and efficiently, and it is the role of the facilitator to ensure that this flexing is managed appropriately and productively. It should be noted that this carries a clear implication for the awareness and competence of the facilitator to introduce a range of viable options within the process. However, the tools are simple and it does not take long for a good facilitator to master them. But, as the old adage says: 'When the only tool you have in your toolbox is a hammer, it is amazing how many of your issues begin to look like nails!'.

The impact of multi-channel events

From all of the foregoing, it can be seen that assured success in using a multi-channel approach carries quite a responsibility for those designing and running such meetings. The professionalism referred to at the start of the chapter is a long cry away from the way most managers prepare for their current meetings, so a really good question at this point would be: 'Is it worth it?'.

We explored precisely this question in our survey of managers. We asked managers who had extensive experience of both single-channel and multi-channel approaches in meetings, to compare their experiences of both. The results are shown in the bar chart on the right of the next page.[1]

From this chart it can be seen that multi-channel meetings are almost universally more effective than single-channel meetings in all of the things that we are trying to achieve with a meeting.

[1] Survey data – see Appendix 1, reference point M.

While that seems fairly straightforward, perhaps we could pause here to reflect for a moment, because at one level, to say that multi-channel working achieves the objectives of the meeting is to underplay what the chart is telling us. Please look again at the influence it has on creativity, engagement, energy and enthusiasm, commitment, trust and relationships, and impact.

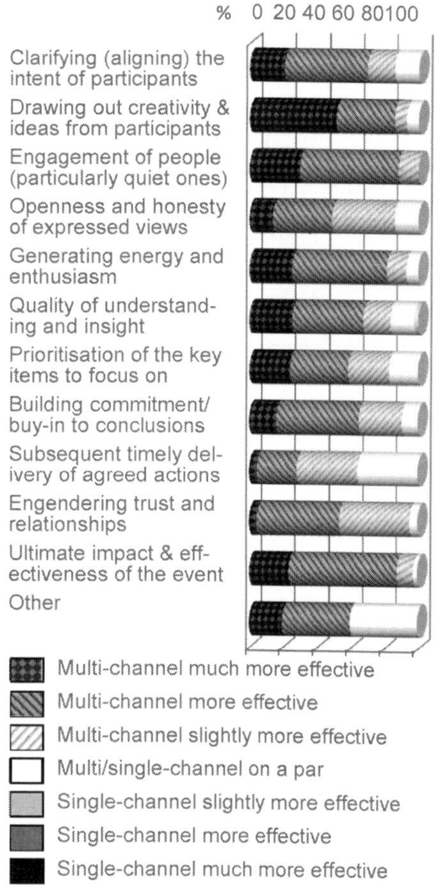

Is this not precisely what we have been seeking? Is this not 'engaging more of the practical creativity and resourcefulness of our people to bring about a step change in performance'?

What we are looking at here is not so much 'an improvement', as the potential to inspire and transform people's working lives!

Issues with multi-channel events

The question which has to be asked is, if they are so much more effective, why are they not more commonly used within organisations? The survey asked this question too, and the results are shown on the opposite page.

Essentially, the key obstacles appear to be:[1]

- Time constraints in setting up and running the meetings
- Attitudes of people, particularly those in senior positions, who may be cynical about the approach, optimistic about how well traditional meetings actually work, or reluctant to give up 'their platform'
- Physical limitations in terms of the appropriate facilities, and the difficulty of setting up the walls.

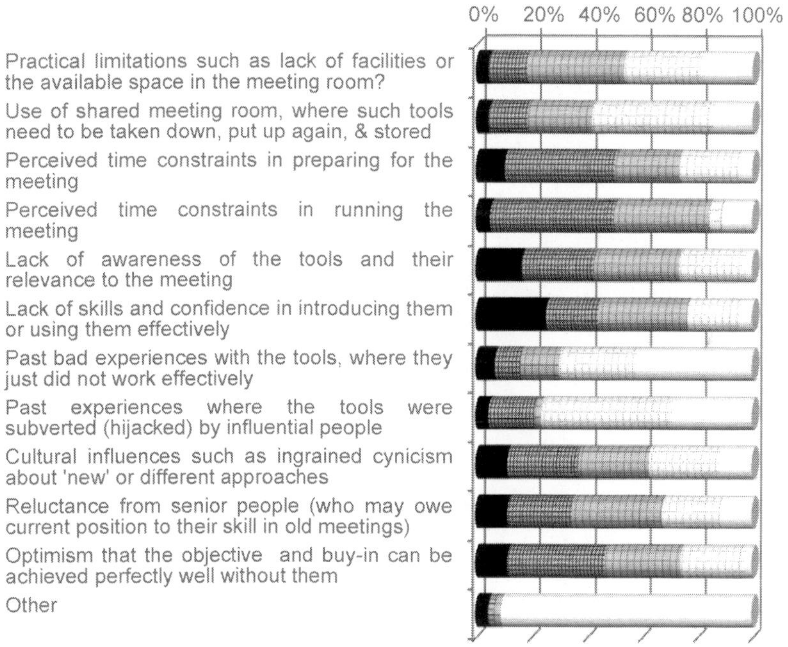

[1] Survey data – see Appendix 1, reference point N

In this chapter we have focused our exploration of best practice very much on workshops because these are the most obvious and rigorous application of multi-channel thinking, but increasingly multi-channel approaches and attitudes are *beginning* to find their way into the mainstream.[1] As yet, this is not widespread, partly because of the issues, but largely because people do not think about it – it is a change and people are happier to flow with the status quo despite the problems.

However, there is a change already on the horizon. A change which will disrupt the status quo, a change that will address a number of the issues outlined above, a change that will make it easier to think of new ways to do things, and remove the patterns which drag us back to traditional practices. We are talking about the emergence of web-based meetings, and we look at the potential for these to bring about a real revolution in meeting design in the next chapter, in Part Two.

In summary

Externally facilitated workshops tend to perform significantly better than meetings conducted in-house, despite taking on more ambitious goals. Key to their success is the extent to which they clarify their impact, embrace process and participation to achieve it, and are managed at the meta-level to ensure there is real commitment to the conclusions.

[1] 18 per cent of meetings do utilise some aspect of concurrent participation within them. Survey data – see Appendix 1, reference point E.

These principles apply equally well to short internal meetings, and there is an economic level of investment in them which will ensure greater progress, more inspired outcomes, and less time wasted.

Insight: Questions for reflection

If you were to compare your most recent meetings against the best practice laid out in this chapter, where would you score most strongly in comparison? And where would be your weak areas?

Where would you say your current project team was in terms of GRIP: Goals, Roles, Interpersonal interactions, and Process?

How often do you use the participative tools outlined on page 102? What stops you using them more?

Part Two

Practical Steps to Fixing the Issue

In Part One we looked at the issues, challenges, and opportunities facing meetings, and discovered that there is a lot more to how meetings work (and how they don't work) than is immediately evident. We concluded, very briefly, with the idea that web-based meetings provide a valid way forward in addressing these issues.

In Part Two, we build on this idea and use the web-based environment as a 'nursery' for developing a best-practice approach to meetings, and a starting point for transplanting those best practices back into our physical meetings.

At first glance, this approach may seem somewhat counter intuitive:

- Web-based meetings, far from reflecting best-practice currently, are actually the nadir of meeting performance

- The web-based environment is comparatively alien and unfamiliar, and very different from the 'normal' meeting environment
- The web is used for just a small proportion of meetings in many organisations, and not for the most important.

But from another perspective, web-based meetings are here to stay, and we begin Part Two by addressing each of these arguments, turning them on their head, and then looking in very practical terms at how it is possible to implement the lessons of Part One, and extend them out to impact all of your meetings.

- Chapter 5 looks at the potential of current developments in web-based technology to deliver multi-channel meetings as part of the everyday working environment. It also looks at the business benefits which are achieved through that
- Chapter 6 introduces some practical steps which can help your organisation to realise these benefits, through adopting multi-channel practices within web-based meetings and gradually establishing the best practice outlined in Chapter 4
- Chapter 7 examines the cultural and organisational implications of ensuring your success in fully realising those benefits, and avoiding two millennia of tradition reasserting itself
- And Chapter 8 gives practical advice on transferring your success in web-based meetings back into the physical environment.

Chapter 5

The Potential of Web-Based Collaboration

In short

In addition to the obvious benefits in making collaboration over distances easier and reducing travel, web-based meetings provide a convenient, economic, and expedient test bed for embedding practices that will radically improve meetings in general.

Given the changes reported in Chapter 3, of the rapid growth in global transactions, and of the level of business travel required to support it, there can be little wonder that there has been so much interest in the concept of web-based meetings. Practically every large organisation now has some sort of web-meeting account with either one of the big players (Microsoft Live Meeting or Cisco WebEx) or with the myriad of smaller businesses that have sprung up to serve this need.[1]

Sadly however, people's average experience of web-based meetings has been largely inferior to their experience of physical

[1] The 2009 Cisco brochure claims that 90 per cent of the Fortune 500 now use their web-based WebEx meeting product.

meetings,[1] and they are reluctant to further reduce their travel because they estimate that the resulting inefficiency and in-effectiveness would, on average, more than three times out-weigh any savings in the travel budget[2] – see diagram on the right.

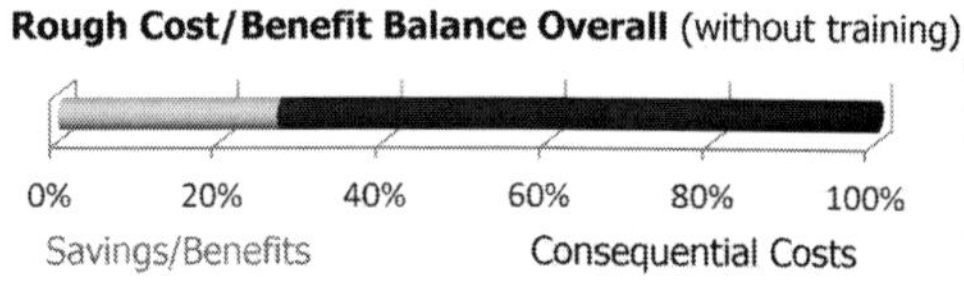

But when you look at how people utilise the functionality available in web-based meetings (or more specifically how they don't utilise it) you can see that most of what can be achieved remains largely dormant and unknown. In fact, the most commonly used features are presentations (including some application sharing) and general discussion. It is fairly clear that what people have done is simply move the traditional way of conducting meetings in the physical environment directly into the web-based environment. Please see diagram on the right.[3]

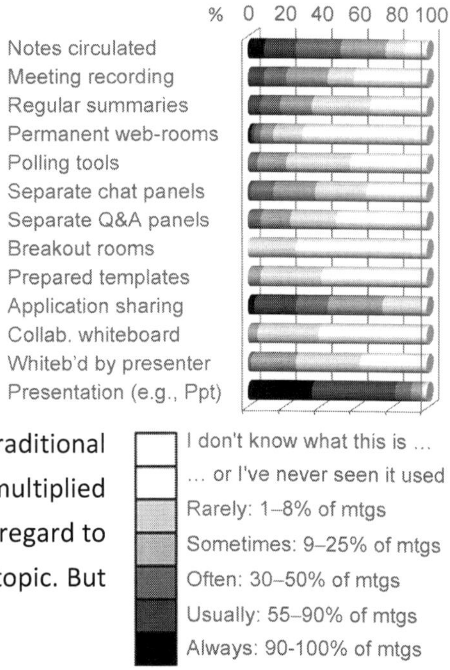

In so doing, they have taken the problems experienced in traditional meetings (see Chapter 2) and multiplied their consequences, particularly in regard to people's disengagement from the topic. But there is a better way.

---

[1] Survey data: Average relative effectiveness 49 per cent – see Appendix 2, reference point T.

[2] Survey data – see Appendix 2, reference point Y.

[3] Survey data – see Appendix 2, reference point U.

The happy coincidence here is that not only are web-based meetings the very opportunity for multi-channel meetings to take a practical place in the mainstream of organisations but, as we will show in this chapter, web-based meetings need multi-channel approaches if they are to effectively achieve their full potential.

It is therefore somewhat ironic that instead of emphasising the range of functionality in web-based meetings, the headlong rush for future development appears to be toward increased bandwidth, better video, and a more realistic representation of people in a room[1] – a strategy which at best can only remain inferior to the physical meetings which they are so determinedly trying to better emulate.

Over the last 30 years of computerising business processes, the one overwhelming lesson (a lesson which has cost millions of hours and billions of pounds in the learning, and now thankfully appears to be enshrined in every significant ERP or SAP implementation) is to refine the process and ensure it is working correctly before it is incorporated into the software. And yet, as we seek to engage with a 'computerisation' of meeting processes, this lesson has been forgotten.

We have *not* clarified our objectives for the meeting process, we have *not* refined the processes by which it takes place, and we have *not* trained our people on the best approaches. We have simply, and largely unthinkingly, attempted to force fit our current, and deeply flawed, practice[2] into the new environment. The

[1] 'The Top 15 Technology Trends EA Should Watch: 2011 To 2013', Leganza, Forrester Research, 2010.
[2] See Chapter 2.

consequences of this actually exacerbates the issue and creates a grossly inferior solution.

If instead of accepting web-based meetings as inferior forms of a flawed process, we take them on their own merits, they actually provide an excellent environment to tackle the issues anew. But this means going back into what meetings really require, and how we can use the web-based environment to computerise the best-practices discussed in Chapter 4, rather than the poor practices discussed in Chapter 2.

In this chapter we will look in some detail at how the web-based meetings environment:

- Provides a varied, exciting, and continuously evolving environment for supporting Tag Meetings
- Enables process to be both easier to implement, and less intrusive (almost transparent) in its execution
- Supports the role of the facilitator both in their awareness of the patterns emerging at the meta-level and in their ability to influence them, particularly in respect of Tackle Meetings
- Provides a mechanism in which it is easier for an organisation to measure and manage the quality of their meetings right through the organisation
- Provides a new environment which helps break the psychological reinforcement of old patterns of behaviour.

We will also explore a number of issues in ensuring that people get the very best out of these opportunities. We will look at:

- The importance of body language and how this relates to effective use of web-based meetings

- The business case of travel-based savings and how this provides a springboard for implementation
- The need to start small, and gradually build and extend this new way of working across the organisation
- The functionality that is available in web-based meetings to support what you are trying to do.

The epitome of 'Tag'

The whole idea behind the World Wide Web is the epitome of 'Tag'. From its earliest beginnings of basic communication, to its collaborative development, through techniques like IRC (Internet Relay Chat), email, bulletin boards, web-pages, blogs, tweets, wikis, remote sharing and the cloud, 'Tag' has been its *raison d'être*. It is designed to exchange, share, store, access, promote, and integrate information; from its earliest incarnation, constrained to basic text, through to its current manifestations of images and expression.

And all the time it is continuing to develop in this role. Every day brings a new development, and the boundaries of what is possible are continually moving outwards, and are even beginning to embrace the rudiments of Artificial Intelligence:[1] scanning for the events we have an interest in, and delivering our more routine responses on our behalf.

Increasingly this electronic Tag world is becoming part of our working (and our private) lives, as different offerings on the web

[1] At the time of writing, a website called ifttt.com (if *This* then *That*) scans periodically for events (*This*) and responds in a user-defined manner (*That*) when it encounters them.

integrate the various aspects of this new functionality – a prime example of which is the emerging 'Always Connected' solution.

But to what extent do we proactively consider the most productive ways to integrate these things into our work patterns, and how best to exploit their potential? Or to what extent are we the flotsam on the wave, carried along passively and picking up only the obvious and inevitable?

To be fair, many IT policies would have proved a major obstacle to a proactive approach in the past, but these are now beginning to change, and we are seeing increased acceptance of the need to embrace developments and the adoption of BYO (Bring Your Own Computer to Work) policies.

It is now time to re-examine your Tag needs and to reconsider the potential of such tools as blogs, wikis, forums, cloud sharing, scrapbooks, and how they might be used; used not only to substitute for some physical meetings, but also to stem the overuse of other tools such as email. The internet carries huge under-utilised potential for Tag.[1] But it also, through some of its more sophisticated developments, provides tremendous potential for Tackle as well, not least in terms of how easy it is to ensure both quality and flexibility of process within the current web environment.

The inherency of process

In the physical world, many meetings take place as a matter of course, without people seriously thinking about how, when, and

[1] For further information on this, please see Appendix 8.

where they will take place or who will attend them.[1] Others are often a response to an emerging issue: 'Right, we'd better get together with Sue and Joe, and someone form Marketing; I'm free on Wednesday at three? Here? OK, let's go for that then!'.

The very process of setting up a web-based meeting automatically imposes a modicum of rigour: logging in, defining a title, selecting attendees, setting times, choosing options, uploading materials. Agreed, it is not a lot (the software developers try to keep it as simple and as painless as possible) but it does take people to a place where thinking about process is an easy next step, and that is a welcome development in a world where introducing process to a meeting is somewhat counter-cultural.

And once people have decided that they may want to add in a little bit more process, it is surprisingly easy to do; as easy as uploading a presentation in fact. In physical meetings, using wall space usually involves taking down pictures, and sticking up yards of brown paper (which of course can't be found because it gets used so rarely), and creating templates for people to engage with involves subcontracting the work to someone with an A1 printer (who can't actually get it done in time for the meeting). But web-based meetings deliver 'wall space' and iFrames (web-based templates) on-demand, with a few clicks of the mouse. White-boards can be set up in mass profusion (and even given specific names) and attractive, engaging iFrames, to support any manner

[1] Survey data: 39 per cent of meetings take place without any clear need, simply because they are scheduled to – see Appendix 1, reference point C.

of discussion tools and meeting processes, can easily be selected and uploaded to your meeting.[1]

Unlike physical meeting rooms, people working in a web-based meeting are not constrained by wall-space.[2] Their room is of virtually infinite size, and they can set up as many iFrames and white-boards as they require. Each iFrame can be the equivalent of about 5m high and 5m wide but, unlike the physical world, people do not need a stepladder to work on it. And as many people can crowd round each of the displays as wish to, without obscuring anybody else's view or getting in the way of their contribution.

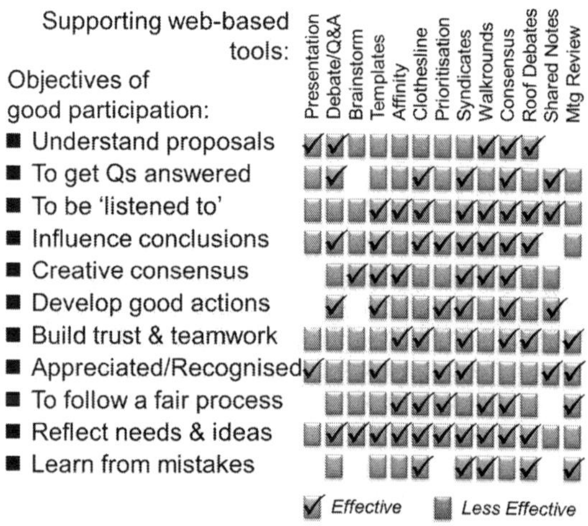

What is more, all of this can be set-up in about five minutes with no help from maintenance, and it can be taken down in the same time. However, people actually have no need to take down the materials because the room is there for as long as they want it to be, meaning people can visit it and refresh their understanding, contributing new things whenever appropriate. It will all be there, as they left it, when the team go back in for a follow-up meeting.

[1] See Appendix 4 on iFrames.

[2] 53 per cent of people stated that availability of appropriate facilities was a significant barrier to multi-channel meetings. Survey data – Appendix 1, reference point N.

Furthermore, since people can update, prepare, and review things outside of the formal meeting, and since nobody has to leave their desk, a follow-up meeting can be as short as a five-minute check to see that everybody has read and responded to the developments, progress is on track, and there are no issues – all quick and visual with no attendant waffle and time-filling.

If the iFrames are well designed, the process feels as natural as any interaction through a computer screen can feel (and even that feels increasingly natural)[1] and people will not even realise that they have been part of a process.

Perhaps as the final reflection of the ease of process in a web-based meeting: there is no gathering, ordering, and annotating of a pile of flipchart sheets for a beleaguered assistant to type up and circulate.

Facilitating facilitation

Since good process is more than half the battle in effective facilitation, we are already off to a fine start. But the web-based meeting environment has even more features available, which can make web-based facilitation surprisingly easy.

Perhaps the most valuable of these, and the most under-used, is the ability to be in several places at once. When physical meetings break out into syndicate rooms (for instance to work on different aspects of the problem in parallel sub-teams) it is difficult to keep an overview on the progress of all the sub-teams at once. But in a

[1] 71 per cent of UK households now have a computer with internet access. Source: 'Living Costs and Food Survey', Office for National Statistics, 2009.

web-based meeting it is simply a matter of opening a window onto each one and arranging them so that the organiser can see them all at the same time.

Of course, implicit in the last paragraph is that, unlike the physical world, having break out rooms at your disposal is an ever present and easy to access possibility. And bringing them all back on time to the main meeting room is as easy as a single click.

Apart from the main screen, and further windows onto the breakout rooms, there are other means of developing an overall picture of what is emerging and how people feel about it:

- There is of course the audio channel
- There is also the opportunity to mute audio and drive all input to typed contributions so that the development of the debate is more visual
- Contributions to iFrames and whiteboards can either be colour coded to see the balance of inputs and where they come from, or they can be 'hovered over' to identify the source
- The chat facility can be used to handle concerns outside of the main forum, without distracting other participants
- Avatars can be used on iFrames so that people can reflect changing perspectives, and the facilitator can observe the flow toward or away from consensus
- Polls are quick and easy to set up to assess positions on the process, and to ensure full engagement
- There is a simple means for people to highlight issues or flag up a response, and for this to be assessed over the group.

Although web-based meetings lack the ability for the facilitator to observe actual body language as a back-channel, the range of multi-channel options which exist can, when used appropriately, more than compensate for this shortcoming.

All the foregoing just covers the facilitator's options for observing the patterns; their scope for influencing the patterns is greater still:

- 'Permissions' can be set for the participants to allow them access to different aspects of the functionality at different times: chat, audio, annotation, shared notes, ability to change content, etc.
- People can transfer to and from break out rooms almost instantly
- Individuals can be communicated with personally and individually, without disturbing the main flow
- The focus of attention can be shifted as required
- iFrames can be easily created and/or uploaded to guide inputs in the most appropriate way
- Content can be moved or adjusted as required
- Latecomers can be merged into the meeting at the most appropriate point and with a minimum of disruption.

Utilised as part of a designed process, or adjusted as required to keep the process on track, these tools provide far more practical influence than is normally afforded a facilitator in a physical meeting. With careful and appropriate application, these controls can be accepted by participants as an expected and integral part of the process, and this provides a real opportunity to address some of the unproductive meeting behaviour issues flagged up in Chapter 2.

Not least among these issues is the imbalance of input in most meetings, and the dominance of the meeting by those who are more vociferous and demanding. Keeping a balance of input, and ensuring more reflective members of the meeting are properly heard and understood, has always been a challenge for facilitation. But in the web-based environment, everybody has a keyboard and a mouse and full access to the content of the screen. Quiet, reflective types have the same font sizes and space as those who are more immediate and forcible in their opinions. Furthermore, input is taken and evaluated on its merit rather than on its decibel level. As a result, it is much easier to 'engage the practical creativity and resourcefulness' especially of those who are more inclined to think than to talk, and thereby increase the probability of 'bringing about a step change in performance'.

Are quieter people more likely to take this opportunity? Almost certainly. Not least because they don't have to fight for it, and they don't have to compete in terms of volume and emotion. But also because it is easier for the facilitator to monitor the balance of input, to encourage in the background, and ultimately to address inappropriate behaviours (e.g., dominant, non-contributory) over a period of time, as we will see the next section.

Ease of review

Future Coaching?

Imagine, you are in a coaching session and your coach says to you, 'Do you feel that the directness of your approach can sometimes have a negative influence on those around you?' And you say, 'Well, I'm not sure, why?' She replies, 'I was thinking about the meeting last week and your response to Adam's point on XYZ!' You puzzle, 'I can't really remember.' To which she responds, 'Well, let's dip back into the meeting and take another look at what happened...'

Have you ever heard of a coaching session like the one on the right? Probably not, but it is a very real option with web-based meetings. Every single meeting has the ability to be recorded and the result stored online (or locally) for a period of up to a year. This gives the chance for people who missed the meeting to catch up with what went on (and how it went on) or for others to go back and remind themselves of the reason for a particular decision. But it also gives the facility for people to:

- Review what went wrong in their meeting and so improve future events
- Assess trends in the performance and quality of meetings within the organisation
- Address instances of counter-productive behaviour
- Reward and share models of productive behaviour
- Enable peer review and coaching of attendees, leaders, and facilitators.

The web-based environment not only provides better facilities for review and control of meetings from within the meeting itself, it also provides for review and control of meetings from a corporate perspective – an opportunity to better understand and influence what is essentially *the* most important and time consuming plank of management.

Furthermore, the web-based environment provides for easier collective and individual assessment of meetings across a range of criteria, and for the collation and analysis of this data at an organisation level, so that the meeting process as a whole may be improved. It is surprisingly easy to end a web-based meeting with a web page which is a short survey of how well the meeting met its objectives (including those of commitment and culture), and it is surprisingly easy to collate and analyse these responses to observe trends and patterns and the root causes that underlie them. For further information on such review tools see Appendix 14.

The advantages of a different environment

Attending a meeting through web-based software is different to people's normal experience of meetings. A lot of the tools and iFrames are not familiar, and people have to pause to think about how to use them rather than simply leap in. Many have simply fallen into using the software with very little training, and are aware that there is a lot more functionality available than they are actually using, and so they do not feel 100 per cent confident in what they are doing.

At one level, this 'alien' sense of the meeting environment might be seen as a disadvantage, but in a situation where you are seeking to change a long-established, traditional attitude and approach into a new, multi-channel mindset, an unfamiliar environment can be a big advantage. To understand why, it is helpful to turn to a branch of psychology called Neuro-linguistic Programming (NLP).

NLP is an effective way of recognising the influences on behaviour and changing them. One of the key tools within this approach is 'triggers', where people work to associate feelings inside themselves with sensory cues. This is actually a natural effect which happens automatically in most of us; if you are attuned to what is going on inside you, you will notice it when you step into a room in which you have had either good or bad experiences, or where you expect to do so. Try stepping onto a big stage in an empty auditorium and turn your awareness to what is going on inside yourself. Your feelings at this point are an association, and what NLP seeks to do is to change unhelpful associations to helpful ones.

Physical meetings have similar associations. Some things feel natural and expected within them, and some feel unnatural and alien. Let us look at these two different types of feelings.

With respect to things in the former category (things that feel natural and expected in physical meetings), some of these are actually detrimental to what we are trying to achieve. For instance, automatic responses when people feel the discussion is not going their way:

- Some (usually more senior) people try to dominate the meeting, even to the extent of subverting or disqualifying the process if necessary

- Others disengage from the process – they distance themselves from what is going on, waiting for it to fail.

Things in the latter category (that feel unnatural and alien) tend to involve an uphill struggle – people are expecting resistance to them, and the feelings they have inside themselves, and the feelings they induce in other people are not always the most conducive to delivering success.

Sadly, most of the practices we have described in multi-channel meetings would fall into this latter category. Conducting them in an off-site workshop, in a different environment, with a confident professional facilitator who everybody expects to do things differently, may not generate too much natural resistance. But there is still psychological resistance to overcome for Joe Soap to introduce them into the normal working environment,[1] and usually that resistance is just enough to deter people, particularly when they themselves are not 100 per cent confident in the tool.[2]

The exception to this is when people are looking to do something different; when they *need* to do something different. For instance, try suggesting using web-based meeting software for a meeting where everyone is physically present anyway, and you will be unlikely to succeed. But try suggesting it for a meeting where one or two key people cannot physically be present, and acceptance is much more likely. And once people are in the web-based environ-

[1] 63 per cent of managers believe that ingrained cynicism is a significant obstacle to the adoption of multi-channel tools, and 67 per cent believe that senior management reluctance would be a significant factor in them not being used more widely. Survey data – see Appendix 1, reference point N.

[2] 77 per cent of survey respondents cited 'lack of confidence in their ability to use the tools effectively' as a significant factor in not introducing them as part of meetings. Survey data – see Appendix 1, reference point N.

ment, they are already accepting that the things they do within that will be different.

The visual cues in the new environment will be fresh, waiting for participants to associate new feelings and behavioural responses with them. The sensory cues in physical meetings which work against the 'intrusion' of new methods will be less prevalent. With careful selection of the process, triggers for dominance or disengagement can be avoided (or their responses contained) and the new tools can succeed or fail by their own merits.

And who knows, as people become more familiar with the new environment, and new and more productive triggers are written within it, maybe the suggestion to hold a web-based meeting even though everybody is physically present may not seem so alien after all.

As one participant at a web-based meeting put it: 'It definitely adds additional dimensions to meeting (especially compared to teleconferences) – almost feels like comparing radio and television with added "picture"; or even better, to a play in a theatre where we are not the audience but actors.'

And from the perspective of another: 'It gave us all the opportunity to take an active role in the meetings. It was good to be able to see so much data and feedback on one screen. It was a good way to capture and record our thoughts and ideas without having to "wait our turn".'

The body language issue

Perhaps the biggest objection that people have to using web-based meetings comes from the idea that they are not suitable for building relationships. While there is an element of truth in this, the majority of feelings in this regard have arisen from un-questioned myths concerning the nature of relationships.

A majority of people appear to believe that the need to see body language and watch facial expressions is paramount in building a relationship. They believe that it is through these that you can tell whether or not you can trust them. And it is true; it is possible to tell through these things. But the myth is that we have the skill to be accurate in such judgements. The truth, for many of us, is that we more usually arrive at our judgements based on what people say and do, and then rationalise this back to their posture. Yes, there are cues that our subconscious picks up, but in our normal working environment these are unlikely to be conclusive, and can lead us as often into a wrong perception as a right one. Only in the extremes does this intuition work for us, and even then we are far more likely to confirm untrustworthiness in how we are treated, rather than how the person looks at us.

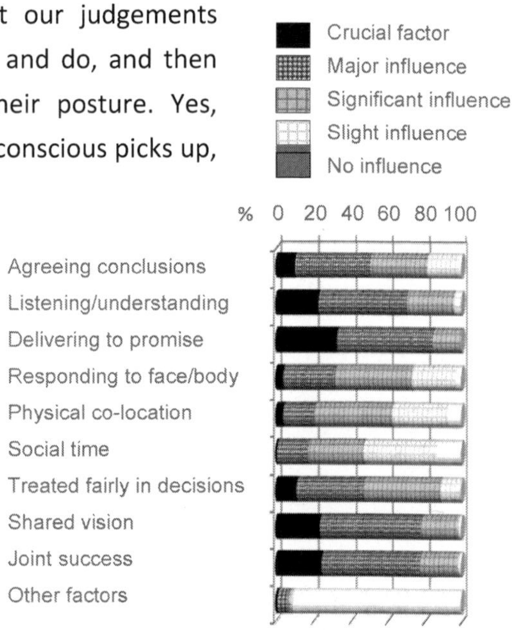

To illustrate this, we surveyed a cross-section of managers on the key factors that led to them building relationships with people. We asked them to reflect on specific people that they had met recently in meetings, and whether or not they trusted them. We then asked them to consider the biggest factors involved in building on those relationships, either to overcome mistrust, or to build where there is trust. The results are shown in the chart on the right of the preceding page.[1]

From this, you can see that the biggest factors are delivery, shared vision, joint success, fairness, and agreed conclusions. And the factors which we might naturally assume will be most influential, such as co-location, social time, and body/face language (which are only practically achieved in physical meetings) are actually the least influential.

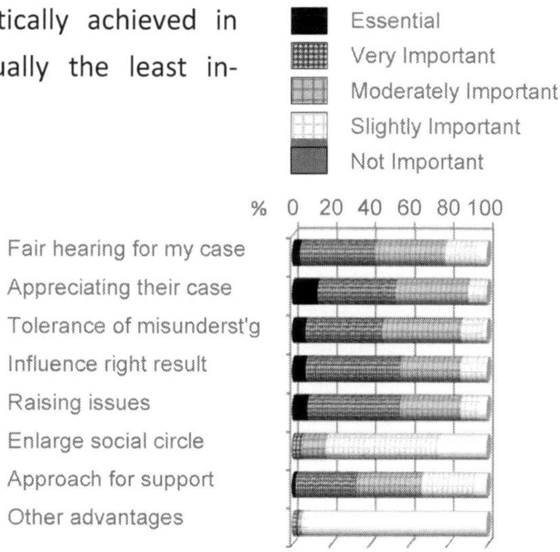

We went on from this to ask people why relationships with people in the work environment were important to them, and the results are shown in the chart on the right.[2] What is interesting is that the most important needs of relationships are those needed to maintain effective influence in traditional meetings, and may even be considered superfluous in the processes of multi-channel meetings.

[1] Survey data – see Appendix 1, reference point O.
[2] Survey data – see Appendix 1, reference point P.

The argument being floated here is that the biggest reservations against web-based meetings, and the biggest justifications for huge financial outlays on large format video conferencing facilities, appear largely based on a myth.

That said, it is still important for people to meet physically; not for every meeting, perhaps, but at least once or twice. Despite the earlier arguments, there is something not entirely rational – or to be more accurate, not *yet* rational within our current understanding of science – about the influence and importance of physical contact. While it does not clearly figure in the charts laid out on the preceding pages, there is something in our subconscious which tells us that it is still important, and we should not ignore this. The jury is still out on whether this is fulfilled by large format video screens.

There is an aspect of body language which is useful and does not directly pertain to relationships; the technique of using it to gain feedback on how people are receiving what you are transmitting. This is particularly important in single-channel meetings where body language is often the only viable and polite back-channel for communicating your immediate response to what is being said. However, in multi-channel meetings, this need is not so evident, for two reasons: 1) There are numerous parallel channels and back-channels that can be used to communicate responses, and these are far more direct and unambiguous, and 2) There is less sense of 'the person who has the floor carries the meeting', and people are inherently more cognisant, largely through the prominence of process, that there are a number of steps between what is being communicated and what is being decided. The photograph on the next page illustrates the fact that in most multi-

channel meetings, people are rarely watching each other's body language since their views are very evident in their contributions to the process. However, we are not saying that video is superfluous in web-based meetings, only that its role is nowhere near as important as it is in single-channel meetings. As bandwidth continues to increase, we look forward to a time when we can utilise the functionality in web-based meetings *and* see everybody's faces as we do so, but in the meantime our argument is that if it is a trade-off between the functionality and the video, then from the perspective of meeting effectiveness and organisational performance, functionality wins hands down.

The business case

In isolation, despite obvious benefits, the migration to increased utilisation of multi-channel techniques is a difficult sell. There is clearly an outlay of time and money involved in building the skills necessary to use the new techniques confidently and consistently well, and there are clearly benefits to be gained from more accurate decisions, with greater commitment, and better influence on culture and developing talents. But all of these benefits are inherently intangible, and the linkage to the resulting cost savings, performance improvement, and sales growth, while potentially massive, is always open to (mis)interpretation and challenge. In other words, while chief executives may be seeking to '[engage] more of the practical creativity and resourcefulness of their people' they would be hard pressed to prove a direct and quantified causality between the mechanisms which support this and a 'step change in performance'. At times of increased financial pressure, management tends to opt for more obvious and direct linkage to cost savings. But here again, the potential of web-based collaboration provides a welcome opportunity.

To summarise the current situation, on an *average* annual basis: [1]

- Managers spend 891 hours to attend 64 meetings at a distance from their place of work, at a direct cost of £19,488 in travel expenses and a further indirect cost of £14,162 due to inefficiencies inherent in working while travelling[2]
- 53 per cent of managers would like to reduce their travel to some degree, and a further 44 per cent would be reluctant for it to increase, despite increasing globalisation. 36 per cent experienced tensions at home as a result of the amount they're travelling[3]
- People's experience of web-based meetings is that they are only 50 per cent as effective as physical meetings in achieving what is needed,[4] and that the average meeting tends to be significantly worse than a physical meeting in terms of the commitment generated[5]
- While many are under budgetary pressure to move significantly more of their travel to virtual meetings of some kind, managers are generally reluctant to do this on the basis that

[1] Based on the overall results of a survey into people's experiences of travel and web-based meetings – see Appendix 2.
[2] Survey data – see Appendix 2, reference point R.
[3] Survey data – see Appendix 2, reference point S.
[4] Survey data – see Appendix 2, reference point T.
[5] Survey data – see Appendix 2, reference point X.

the resulting inefficiencies would outweigh several times over any savings gained in travel costs[1]

- 54 per cent of managers are totally unaware of at least half of the functionality that is available to them in conducting their meetings, and 64 per cent of people leading web-based meetings have had no formal training whatsoever.[2]

However, when managers are more aware of what can be achieved using multi-channel approaches within web-based meetings, and how the previously undiscovered functionality can support that, their views about the potential of web-based meetings begins to shift. Once they understand what is possible they begin to think about the positive implications, and the chart on the right illustrates their responses to how they would hope to utilise this approach, and what they would hope to achieve out of it.[3]

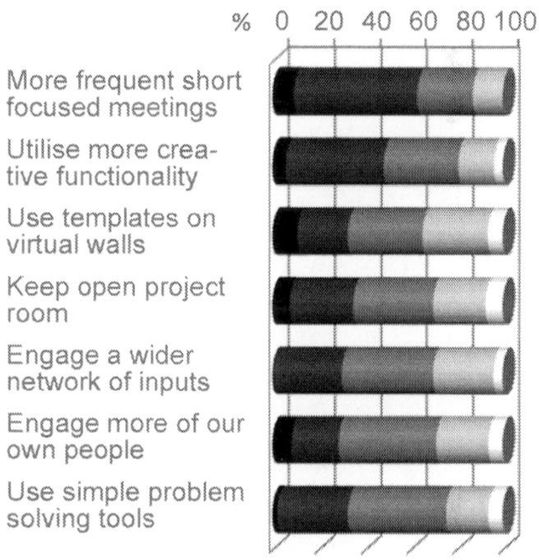

When asked how much travel they would willingly move to such an environment, the average response was 50 per cent, and they would expect that 'move' to bring further benefits in the performance of those meetings.[4] But ignoring the performance impact, which we have already explained is a hard sell in business

---

[1] Survey data – see Appendix 2, reference point Y.
[2] Survey data – see Appendix 2, reference point U.
[3] Survey data – see Appendix 2, reference point W.
[4] Survey data – see Appendix 2, reference point X.

case terms, the cost-savings impact alone of moving half of all travel to web-based meetings represents a very attractive and direct business case.

The savings generated by a 50 per cent migration from travel to web-based meetings represents an average hard saving of £9,744 and 445 hours per annum per manager. Even allowing around £2,500 and *c*.40 hours per head in training costs for the skills necessary to ensure performance benefits are realised, this represents 390 per cent ROI in the first year alone – breakeven almost within the first quarter, whilst still retaining 50 per cent of the travel to address the more intangible aspects of relationships and international culture. Furthermore, the time taken up in preparing properly for web-based meetings, even though it is justified by the impact it will have, actually represents a saving in time over the hours that would otherwise be consumed in travel.

The consequential benefits would be much greater still. How do you evaluate the benefits of increased commitment, delivery of actions on time, a 50 per cent reduction in the meetings that are actually necessary, increased creativity? What would you channel these things into? And what would be the tangible benefits in sales, brand, and finances that would result?

There is of course a multitude of other benefits: 17 tonnes of carbon saved per person per annum, better work/home life balances, better health due to reduced stress, opportunities to engage more partners and business experts at a distance, increased levels of home working, improved development of people's potential, better control of a positive culture.

You don't even need to put a price on these things, because you have already justified your investment in cost savings alone. It feels a little bit like convicting Capone on a tax issue, but sometimes it's just easier that way.

Starting small

However, amidst all of this enthusiasm, it is important to offer a word of caution. While the destination of this journey may be clear and exciting, the steps to arrival may not be quite as obvious as they first appear. There is a huge prize to be gained, but we need to tread carefully to make sure that each step we take is based on good foundations.

No two organisations are the same, and although the average picture demonstrates that there are clear benefits, there are also large variations in the data about how those benefits might best be attained. Furthermore, we are attempting to address decades of tradition and established mind-sets, and that needs to be done with a great deal of care and consideration, particularly when those mind-sets are likely to be 'most established' among senior management. Simply plunging headlong into the opportunity with a standard solution could leave you frustrated and confused about what actually went wrong.

This then is the final area in which web-based meetings provide us with the opportunity to do things in an advantageous way. We are *not* changing the meeting culture of the organisation, we are merely piloting a new way of utilising the potential of web-based meetings, and then rolling it out as appropriate. If we are right in what we believe about the potential of multi-channel meetings, and if we can establish 'meetings for which you would otherwise travel' as the nursery in which that understanding can grow and prove itself, then the rest will take care of itself – its potential will not be constrained for long.

What we propose then is:

- You survey your own organisation (at least in part) to assess where it is similar and where it is different to the averages described in this book[1]
- You identify in which area of the organisation the multi-channel approach to web-based meetings is likely to have the biggest success as an alternative to travel
- You baseline their current situation
- You train people in facilitating multi-channel meetings using the extended functionality available in web-based meetings
- You agree, as part of this training, their strategy for using the multi-channel approach and gaining the organisational benefits from it
- You review the current performance against your baseline
- You use the learning and experience (what went well, and what didn't go so well) to extend the strategy wider in the organisation as appropriate.

Further guidance on those steps can be found in Appendix 5.

[1] Guidance on surveying your organisation can be found in Appendix 3.

The current functionality of web-based collaboration

The list of vendors who provide web-based meeting software is continuing to lengthen. Among them, the two vendors who are currently most evident are Microsoft with their Live Meeting platform (currently evolving into Office Communicator and Lync), and Cisco who now own the WebEx product.

Different vendors provide different functionality in different ways, but in this section we will look at the most prevalent and useful elements of functionality. Diagrams have been included to illustrate Live Meeting's implementation of the functionality, but in many cases this will not be too dissimilar to the way other vendors have incorporated it into their own products. However, the situation is changing all the time, and before committing to a web-based software license, we would recommend that you confirm that it has the functionality that you are looking for. Most vendors offer a trial period with their software to enable you to check these things. The diagram above represents a typical Live Meeting screen as the presenter would see it, and the functionality is accessed predominantly through the menu bar (top left of the screen).

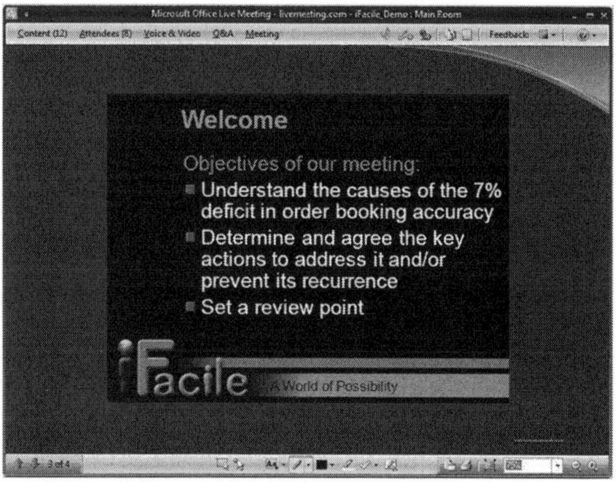

In a (reasonably) logical order, the key elements of functionality are:

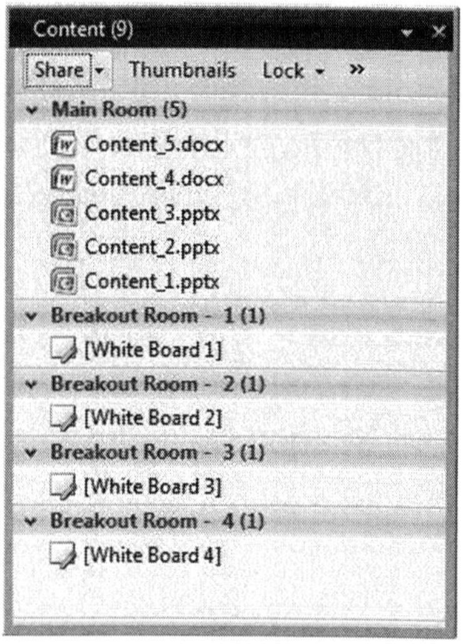

- **Content management** – the facility to have multiple resources to hand, to access them quickly and easily, and to reorganise them as needed. From here, you can normally upload new documents during the meeting, or create new whiteboards as needed
- **Participant management** – the facility to quickly review who the participants are, to see any salient factors in their situation, and to assign them relevant permissions. From here, new participants can be invited (normally by sending them an email with a link to the meeting) and people can be moved to and from break-out rooms, or addressed individually through the chat facility

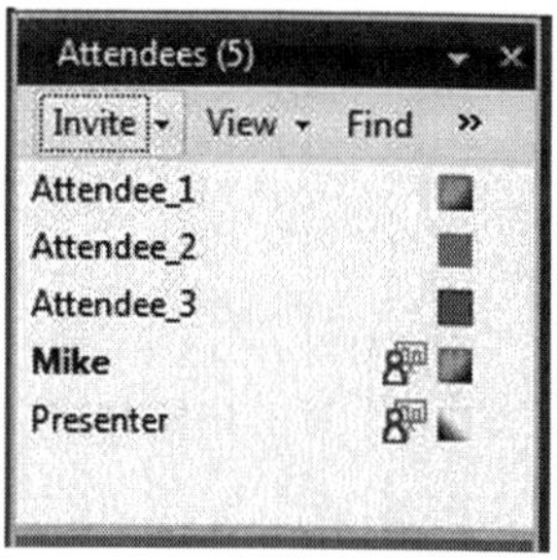

- **Audio and video management** – the facility to control who is able to use audio, and which webcam image is displayed. In some software, this can be set to automatically switch to the current speaker; in others you can have several images on the screen at once (this can be more useful to the presenter)
- **Presentation management** – the facility to present a slide show or video presentation to all participants, on their own computer screens at the same time. This is frequently accessed through 'content management' (see above)

- **Application and desktop sharing** – the facility for the presenter (or sometimes another person) to share what is happening on their computer screen with the others in the meeting – sometimes it is also possible to transfer control (for your mouse and keyboard) to others in the meeting so that they can drive the application directly
- **Whiteboard** – the facility for the presenter or other participants to type or draw onto an electronic whiteboard all at the same time. This is normally a white page of restricted size, on which people contribute using the 'annotation tools'
- **Annotation tools** – the facility for the presenter or the participants to use different fonts, colours, markers, and 'stamps' to annotate content (or a whiteboard) within the meeting. Drawing facilities are often limited to simple shapes or free-hand

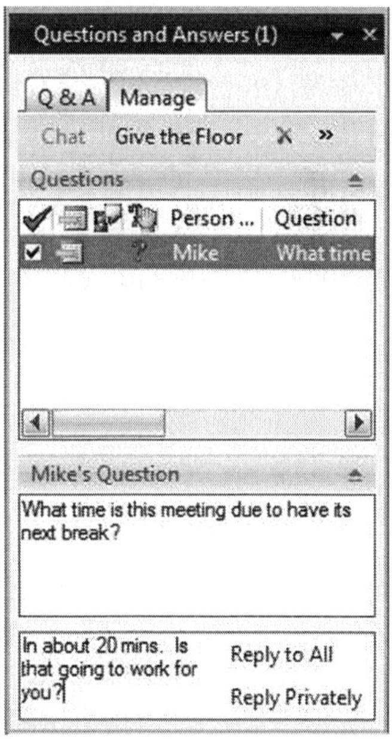

- **Text document** – the facility for the presenter or other participants to type concurrently into a text document at different insertion points
- **Participant chat** – the facility for participants to be able to send each other typed messages without alerting/disturbing other members of the meeting
- **Q&A (question and answer)** – a managed form of chat (see right) where participants can raise questions to presenters (or simply raise 'hands') and the presenters can address them directly or direct their question to other participants/

presenters. This is a very useful tool in managing contributions to a verbal debate, since it stores 'raised hands' in chronological order

- **Status indicator** – the facility for participants to change the colour of their 'marker' to indicate a change in their status, such as 'completed/ready' or 'struggling a bit'. This provides useful feedback to the facilitator which they can see at a glance in the 'participants list' for the meeting, and can therefore manage the timing of activities or direct their attention where it is most needed

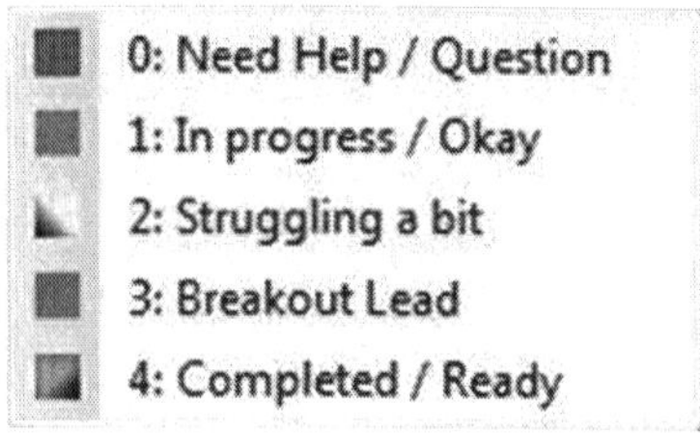

- **Polling pages** – the facility to set up a quick and anonymous poll of participant preferences. The options are usually very limited, and the anonymity limits its usefulness in consensus reaching, but they are useful with very large groups and for a 'quick and dirty' sensing of where people's views stand
- **Content iFrames** – the facility to upload iFrames which participants can use to enter data or perceptions, and come to a conclusion together. In terms of multi-channel meetings, this is pot-entially the most useful feature of web-based meeting soft-ware, but also one of the least emphasised. iFrames can be up-loaded either as slides in a PowerPoint deck (all slides can be annotated) or as individual images. For guidance on using iFrames see Appendix 4

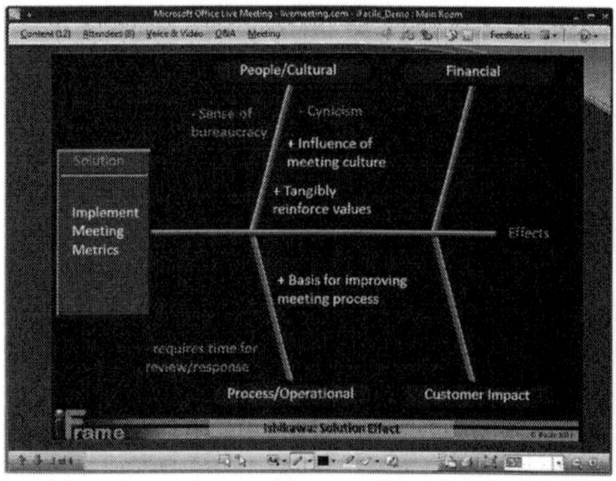

- **Marker iFrames** – the facility to use iFrames in conjunction with markers or avatars to represent positioning within a debate. The approach to uploading marker iFrames is the same as for 'content iFrames'. Avatars are relatively easy to upload in some software (e.g., GoogleDocs) but in others (such as Live Meeting) they can only be achieved currently through using 'Wingdings' icons within the annotation font tool
- **Breakout rooms** – the facility for a meeting to break up into separate groups which can work independently on some aspect of the meeting, and then come back together to share their conclusions. Each breakout room can be furnished with its own content, and changing the focus in one breakout room does not change the focus for others (as it would do if everybody was in the same meeting room)

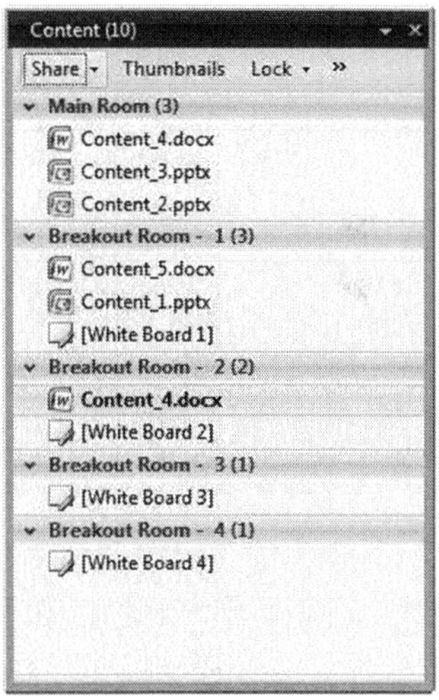

- **Permanent meeting rooms** – the facility to set a meeting as 'on-going' and not be bound by a finish time (this allows participants in the meeting to work asynchronously and either prepare inputs ahead of a synchronous event, or prepare outputs after it). Permanent meeting rooms can have breakout rooms within them
- **Meeting recording** – the facility to keep an online recording of the meeting, either for re-view or for updating new members to the meeting

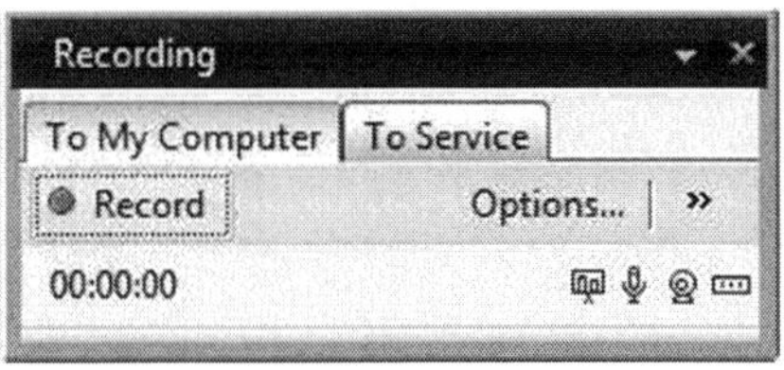

- **Lobby** – the facility to hold attendees in a location before they enter the meeting, either to prepare them with certain information, or (if they are late) to ensure they enter the meeting at the most appropriate point after their arrival
- **Meeting notes** – the facility for participants to summarise the progress of the meeting and develop an ongoing shared log of progress. The fact that they are in a separate window, and that anybody can access them, makes them a useful facility for using as a 'Car Park' for off-topic or 'out of sequence' issues

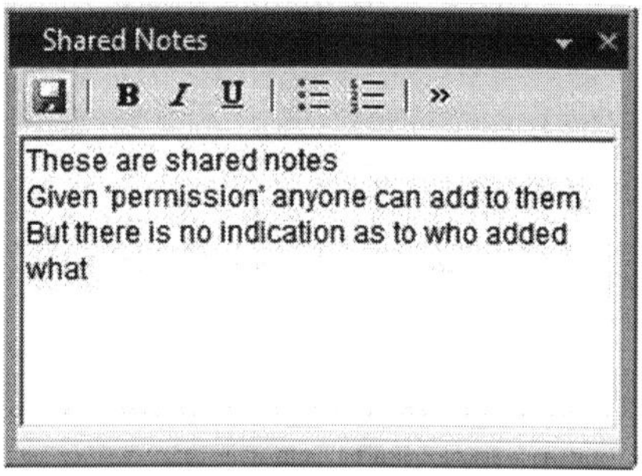

- **Handout management** – the facility for participants to download (or upload) relevant background information or summaries
- **Print management** – the facility to print the annotated content of the meeting as PDFs for future use.

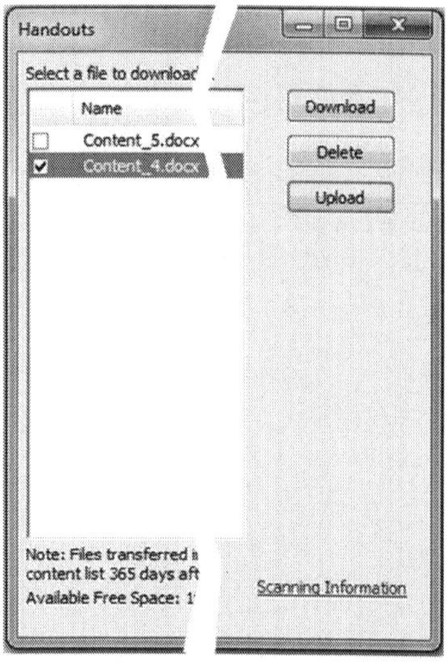

Much of the above may not be immediately obvious to the software user, and some of them need to be configured in the meeting set-up, or switched on as permissions within the meeting. But most of the functionality is there somewhere if you look for it, even if it means using two pieces of web-based software in conjunction with each other.

However, at this point we need to make one huge caveat. As somebody once said, 'To err is human, but to really mess things up, you need a computer!' Their actual words may not have been quite that polite, but they were certainly correct!

Web-based meetings have now evolved to a point where they are a tremendous asset to those who choose to engage with them, and who seek to open-mindedly engage with their potential. But if you are expecting a glitch-free experience, then we are sorry to inform you that you are most likely going to find yourself disappointed. It is relatively astounding that given the sheer number of variables involved from applications, operating systems, hardware, peripherals, TSRs, anti-virals, interfaces, servers, firewalls, routers, ISPs, and other solution providers, that somebody can make something work reliably right across practically all of the viable combinations that are in that space, but they have, and it does – most of the time!

The glitches are now at a manageable level, and the situation will continue to improve, but if you wait until it is perfect, everybody else will have gained the advantages ahead of you. Alternatively, if you are psychologically and practically prepared for the odd glitch then, from this point onwards, we believe that you will reap the benefits and cost-savings that are available to you.

Contrary to popular perception of web-based meetings, they are not only a clear business benefit, but they represent our very best hope of addressing the longstanding issues which we have uncovered in this book, of engaging the very best from our people, of creating a step change in performance and of giving our management the space to think and plan – but the more we proceed with intelligent forethought, the further we will go.

In the next chapter we will explore in a bit more detail the enigmatic phrase from page 142: 'Facilitating multi-channel meetings using the extended functionality available in web-based meetings'. We look at the whole concept of meeting design which lies at the core of this facilitation.

In summary

Web-based solutions have progressed a long way in terms of functionality and reliability, and their potential is advancing.

Engaging with them afresh, on their own merits, provides a practical platform for replicating the very best of meeting thinking.

A big part of your success in this will depend on effective use of the full range of their functionality, and this is likely to require training for your people.

The virtual environment has positive implications for behaviour, for piloting new thinking and for an economic (even cost-saving) solution.

Outworking: How to get started

Open up your preferred web-based meeting software, and look at what is possible within the menus. (If you do not have the software currently, Appendix 7 provides guidance on getting started.)

Explore the developments that support Tag Meetings. Links to some of these can be found in Appendix 8.

Follow the first three steps of the proposal on page 142 (further direct guidance on this can be found in Appendix 5).

Chapter 6

Embracing Process

In short

Efficient meetings require a level of forethought and there are a number of straightforward steps to be taken in preparation for an effective (web-based) meeting, not least clarifying what is to be achieved, and how. And while participative meeting design may (sadly) be a new concept to many managers, there are a number of basic tools to help them to get started.

Concepts like designing a 'flow to the meeting' and 'adapting meeting templates or iFrames' may seem alien to what people see as the management and leadership role. But what is that role if it is not for growing and coordinating the attitudes and abilities of others? And what are meetings if they are not the key channel for practically delivering that role?

The quality of a professional engineer's work is dependent on how well they understand the pattern and interrelationships in the system they are working on. Understanding the flow of what is going on enables them to produce elegant solutions which reflect their expertise. And so they utilise tools such as flow diagrams and graphs to give their minds the best chance of gaining insight and control. A similar picture is true of professionals in medicine, science, etc.

The quality of a professional manager or leader's work is also dependent on 'how well they understand the pattern and inter-relationships' in that work. But, to date, the antiquated nature of meetings (the key channel for delivering leadership and management) has made it difficult for them to 'produce elegant solutions which reflect their expertise'[1] and as a result the emphasis has been more about the 'artistry' of management and leadership than the 'science' of it – and so terms we use in conjunction with the quality of other professionals seem somewhat alien in the management and leadership environment.

But the advent of web-based meetings, and the opportunity to use them as an effective tool to achieve the objectives of professional management and leadership, has the potential to change all that. The purpose of this chapter is to illustrate how; but to be effective it needs to be read from a perspective that wants to properly grasp this new approach; from a perspective that truly seeks to bring more professionalism to the role and recognises that work (some of it alien) will be needed to close the gap. It cannot be read from a perspective which simply sees 'professionalism' as its due.

This may sound a little daunting at first impression, but the advantage which people embracing this new world have is that they are starting from a low base. Success in the first instance is

---

[1] The biggest factor in meeting inefficiency and ineffectiveness (and thereby the results we reviewed in Chapter 2) is meeting design (cited as a significant factor by 83 per cent of respondents). See survey data – Appendix 1, reference point L.

merely improving on what currently exists and, as we have already seen in Chapter 2, there is a lot of scope for improvement. All that we talk about within this chapter are merely options and opportunities for bringing that about, and each can, and should, be used in a manner which sustains the facilitator's confidence, and which is comfortable for the participants to work within.

However, it should be noted from the outset that good meeting design and good meeting facilitation are both skills, and as skills they will take time and practice to master; the different aspects of the skill base need to be assimilated, adapted, and built upon over time as confidence builds. As such, while this book can map out the journey, it is not the journey itself. From the 'map' of these pages, it will be very much a matter of trying things out, getting feedback, adapting your approach, blending new things into it, and moving forward at your own pace.

Our hope is to, as far as possible, equip you for your first few steps in web-based meeting design:

- We will begin where all meeting design should begin, with clarifying the objectives for your meeting
- We will then look at some basic principles of process, and how they influence the design of the meeting
- Our next step will be simply to help you to use these principles to adapt and build on your existing approaches to setting up a meeting. Our hope here is to provide you with a comfortable set of first-steps which you can climb upon as you grow in confidence and ambition

- Process mastery begins to introduce a more systematic approach that will enable you to build on your initial skills, and ensure your continued development and success
- And finally, we look at how all of this gets transferred, in a practical sense, to the web-meeting environment.

It may be obvious from this list that we are focusing in this Chapter more on Tackle Meetings than on Tag Meetings. There are a number of reasons for this:

- Tag Meetings are generally about a simple and straight-forward flow of information
- The need for, and the design of, appropriate Tag Meetings will largely be determined by a well-run Tackle Meeting
- The design of Tag Meetings is largely determined by the medium you choose for running them
- Tackle Meetings are largely where the problem lies in how we run meetings.

Furthermore, if problems exist in Tag Meetings, the consequences tend to be a degree of inefficiency and the issues are easily identified and fixed. Tag Meetings are essentially simple things. Conversely, if problems exist in Tackle Meetings (as they currently do) the consequences are far reaching, and Chapter 2 illustrates that we are poor at identifying and fixing these issues.

But before we move past Tag Meetings entirely, there is one very important piece of process to flag up. Tag Meetings will run simply, providing there is not an unresolved Tackle issue lurking in the wings (see the diagram on page 80), but Tackle issues are not always as obvious as might be imagined. However they are often highlighted by a regular review of how well things are working (for instance GRIP on page 95), and we would recommend that Tag Meetings include such a review (brief and to the point) on a frequent basis.[1]

Clarifying what is to be achieved

At first glance, you might think that 'what is to be achieved' is obvious, but our experience is that this is rarely the case. For instance, look back to the list of objectives on page 53, and take the last example of 'Document the project delivery process'. Looking back at this objective through the lens of the diagram introduced in Chapter 1 (sidebar on page 37) there are a number of questions which emerge:

- Why are we documenting it, and for what purpose?
- How does that purpose add value to the organisation?
- Assuming the deliverable is a document which describes the project delivery process, would any such document do?
- Are there a range of answers for the above questions, and if so, which would represent the best ones?
- Where are we starting from; what already exists that may be a platform to build upon?
- Do the stakeholders and participants in this meeting have different views on the last two questions?
- What is needed to get them to a common view?

These questions illustrate that 'what is to be achieved' in 'documenting the project delivery process' could be a very broad range of options. Failure to realise this, or ignoring the possibility

[1] An example of a Tag review can be found in Appendix 14.

of it, is usually a route to a degree of frustration, and certainly a cause of inefficiency.

If the stakeholders and participants in the meeting (those seeking its conclusions, and those responsible for bringing them about) have different perspectives on the answers to the above questions, then the efficiency of the meeting will depend on them realising this from the outset, and working to reconcile their perspectives into a common view so that one solution can be agreed, and one path defined. Sadly however, many organisations are more familiar with the experience of discovering part way through the process that key people have different assumptions, and then trying to negotiate a pragmatic pathway through compromise. This is commonly serviced by maintaining a degree of ambiguity, which at its extreme can become quite political and results in solutions that nobody is fully happy with.

Efficient design of the meeting is dependent on a clear understanding of exactly what is to be achieved (including, if required, reconciling perspectives within the meeting). This is dependent on answering questions like those on the previous page, and often that means having off-line discussions with the key stakeholders to understand their starting positions on the questions, their reasoning behind these, and their open-mindedness around them. In practice this is far less common in internal meetings than it is in externally facilitated ones but, there again, so are powerful and efficient conclusions.

Principles of process

When organisations are working well, they have a sense of flow. The connections between opportunity and strategy provide confidence and insight; synergies are evident between strategy and management control, and this extends across all the different areas of the organisation so that all of the parts add up seamlessly to one complete whole; and management is in tune with the reality of what is happening on the ground. The organisation seems to hum, and the channels of communication are wide open and full of traffic which moves easily and effortlessly from one level to the next, providing meaning and context in one direction and con-firmation and inquiry in the other.

Like the lifeblood in a living organism, the flow is all important to the health and vitality of both the organisation as a whole and of each individual meeting within it. And when the process becomes broken in some way, because the flow has become restricted or disjointed, then it is the role of management to discern this, to understand the reasons for it, and to prioritise the necessary treatment.

Sadly however, the sense of flow is rarely quite as evident as all this suggests, and management's response to the issues created by problems in the flow is more likely to be about isolated fixes than a systematic dredging of the channels. And, as the channels develop more blockages and fractures, management becomes increasingly tied up in compensating for the problems, with less time available for fixing them at root, until they no longer discern the flow at all.

Please pause here for a moment to allow that idea to bed in. What we are saying is that when organisations are working well, there is a clear sense of flow to them, but when there are issues in the way the organisation is working, that sense of flow will become disrupted. We are also saying that where such disruption occurs, management need to repair the flow through process, or they will end up becoming an integral part of compensating for the disruption through regular fixes, and the sense of flow will be lost. This is not only inefficient, but it is unsustainable – and it is not a particularly pleasant way to work either.

It is clearly therefore incumbent on the manager to recognise where such issues exist, and to set about a chain of events that will reconnect the flow as it should be. In doing this, the manager's key tool is meetings: Tackle Meetings to understand the problems in the flow and to design a solution; Tag Meetings as an efficient conduit to maintain and improve the flow.

This same sense of flow is evident in meetings and projects when they are working well. At one level, clearly defined goals outline the expectations of what the process needs to deliver, which in turn deploys down into the roles and responsibilities of people within that process. And the interpersonal skills sit at the centre and hold the whole thing together.

But good meetings also have a sense of flow within them, and in designing them it helps to be aware of what these flows are.

At another level is Kolb's learning cycle, introduced earlier.[1] If a meeting is to be effective, people need to walk out of it with different understanding and intentions than when they walked in – or at least some of them need to. That is learning at its most fundamental. Learning is something that can take place efficiently (which leads to short and effective meetings) or inefficiently (which leads to prolonged and ineffective ones), and the learning cycle is a big factor in the difference between the two. The principle here is that your meeting is more likely to be effective in making a difference if it gives people a number of opportunities to engage with reality, reflect on what emerges, incorporate this into a valid rationale within their minds, and use this to plan how they will apply it for tangible benefit.

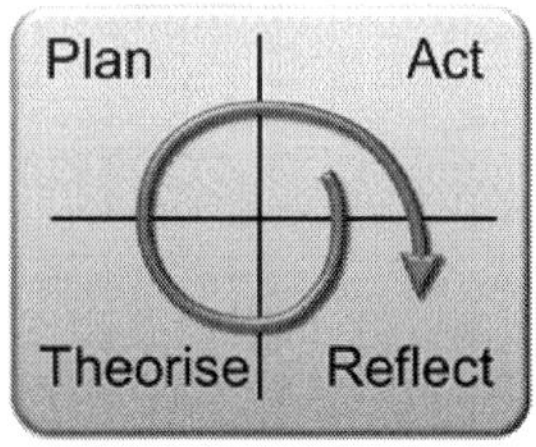

But probably the most definitive flow within meetings is the decision making process itself, which is explained overleaf. Decisions are made at all different levels of detail within a meeting, with bigger decisions comprising of multiple smaller decisions, and so the flow represented on the next page may be a quick flash through, and/or it may consume the whole meeting. In the latter case, you may be able to discern parallels between this flow and the aims of meeting which we developed on page 37.

[1] Chapter 4, page 104.

Sidebar: The decision making process

Decision making, whether individual or collective, appears to be something that we don't 'think about' very often, and yet there is a pattern to it – a sequence of things which take place almost subconsciously (much like Kolb's learning cycle). The diagram below illustrates the general flow. Depending on the decision, we may cycle within it, skip steps entirely, or even repeat the process as a sub-process within itself. If we use the steps well, we will usually make good decisions, and if we use them poorly, we will make bad ones.

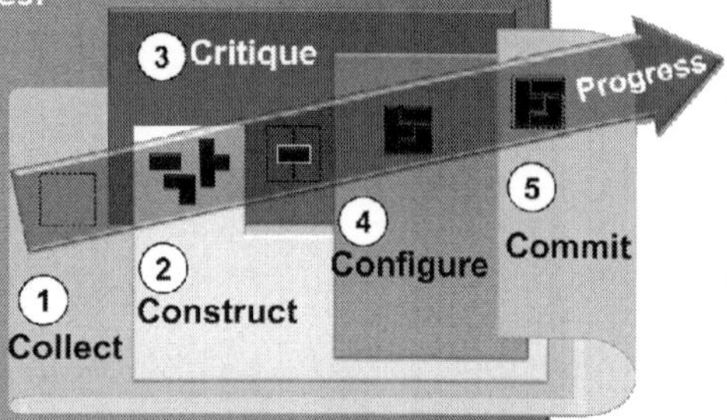

The key steps illustrated are:

1. **Collecting or recollecting** – understanding the current situation in terms of the need, how it is currently fulfilled, and any other salient features of the situation
2. **Constructing possibilities** – considering a range of alternative explanations or ideas – this is a creative step about opening up perspectives on what might be possible
3. **Critiquing what has emerged** – sifting out the valuable possibilities from those that are flawed in some way
4. **Configuring a way forward** – pulling the preferred ideas together into some sort of rationale, or strategy for moving forward – perhaps a critique, or a plan, or a solution
5. **Committing** – making a decision to invest (sacrifice) what is needed to take things to the next step.

Meetings that recognise these flows, which engage and support them, and seek to utilise the natural currents within them, tend to carry their participants on a journey that is relatively harmonious and productive. Combining these flows, (the organisational flows and the flows within meetings) provides a connectedness from the highest ideals of corporate existence right the way through to the choice of an individual's next few words. Recognising that connectedness, reinforcing it, and utilising it, is both an art and a science.

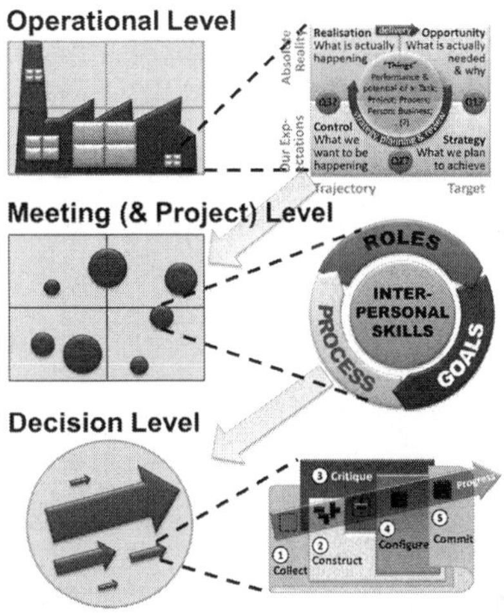

Some practical steps in moving forward

In laying out these steps for moving forward, we need to begin with two basic assumptions:

- You have access to software to run web-based meetings, as do the people you plan to involve in the meetings
- You have familiarised yourself with the key functionality of the software, and have received some basic familiarisation or training in its use.

The wide availability of web-based meeting software leads us to believe that most people reading this book will have access to it within their organisation, and many will also have experience of using it.

If however this is not true for you or your organisation, Chapter 5 and Appendix 7 provides some useful guidance to get you started.

> 'Excellence is a game of inches.'
>
> Tom Peters

We would also like to re-emphasise a point made earlier. Meetings as they currently occur have a lot of problems within them, web-based meetings doubly so, and yet things still continue at current levels of performance. Therefore, in preparing for your web-based meeting, you should not feel a burden to make the meeting perfect (you won't achieve that) but just the opportunity to make it a bit better than it would otherwise have been. There is a wealth of resources to help you to do that, but you do not need to include them all at once.

At the end of the preceding section we referred to the 'flow' as both an art and a science. In helping you to move forward in your use of web-based meetings, we are looking to build your confidence gradually, and so we will take the 'art' route.[1]

The 'art' perspective is more about laying out a palette of colours and a selection of brushes and letting you select whichever you feel drawn to, to apply whenever and wherever you think your work will benefit from them.

But the first consideration in this is the 'principles of process' covered in the preceding section. And the question is, looking at your meeting through the lens of process, can you see which flows are

[1] The 'art' perspective is very much about self-help and building up skills and confidence gradually on a canvas of meetings which already exists. The alternative 'science' approach, while both quicker and more systematic/ comprehensive, is best delivered through a formal training course. If you wish to explore the 'science' approach further, Appendix 12 provides guidance on selecting appropriate training courses.

most relevant to what you are trying to do? Starting from the upper areas of the image on page 161, can you see what purpose your meeting fulfils in sustaining the organisational flow to ensure target performances are achieved? And can you use this insight to define an objective for your meeting which is both SMART[1] and focused on demonstrable benefits? This is the first skill of the artist – the artist's eye – the ability to see into the subject with accuracy and insight. For the manager, this insight comes from not taking things for granted, and from taking the time to ask questions. These questions will also provide insight into the lower areas of the diagram, particularly in respect to issues around commonality of goals, clarity of process and roles, etc. Simply by asking these questions you will gain increasing clarity over what the meeting needs to achieve if it is to be fully successful, and the shape of the meeting will begin to form in your mind.

The second area in which the principles of process can help you is with the idea that the meeting is a journey of learning for the participants involved; the realisation that it is not sufficient to structure the meeting simply to identify the correct answers, if the participants fail to believe them or aren't committed to them.

Our suggested approach to beginning to apply these principles is to pull together the structure of the meeting in whatever ways are familiar to you, but then to review that structure from the perspective of the decision-making flow (shown in the sidebar on page 160) and Kolb's learning cycle. Weigh up the attendees in your mind and think through the journey that they need to go on to reach the right conclusion for themselves. Then consider

[1] See footnote on Page 53

whether the flow of your meeting will take them there, and make adjustments to your structure to accommodate these new insights.

It is possible that developing a flow that will carry people to commitment may take a little more time than a meeting which just generates (or even tells) the answers, and you may be reluctant to invest the extra time. But if this is the case, we would suggest you reflect back to the high percentage of meetings that arise simply due to previous meetings not doing what was needed, or due to people failing to complete their actions (pages 56 and 60). It may be better to set a more limited objective for your meeting and deliver it well, than to attempt to deliver a wider objective when you lack the time to ensure commitment.

> 'Why is it that we can never find time to do things right, but we can always find time to do them twice?'
>
> Source Unknown

Having properly identified your subject and sketched out your canvas, the next step is to select the pigments that you will use to bring the canvas to life. These are the events within your meeting – the exercises and activities which carry people through the decision making process, through the stages of the learning cycle, and arrive at the conclusions the organisation needs with the commitment to ensure they will be delivered. To continue this analogy, we can take the 'black' as being a presentation of some kind, and we can take the 'white' as being an open discussion (the two most prevalent methods of meetings) but in between these are a whole spectrum of tools (some of which are illustrated on page 102) for drawing out experiences, encouraging creativity, managing opinions, and inspiring commitment in your people. To begin with it may be still a matter of a canvas which is largely black and white, with a bit of red here and a bit of blue there, but as you grow in confidence, both in the tools and your facilitation of them, you will begin to produce canvases full of colour, where the black and the white are predominantly used for outlining and highlights.

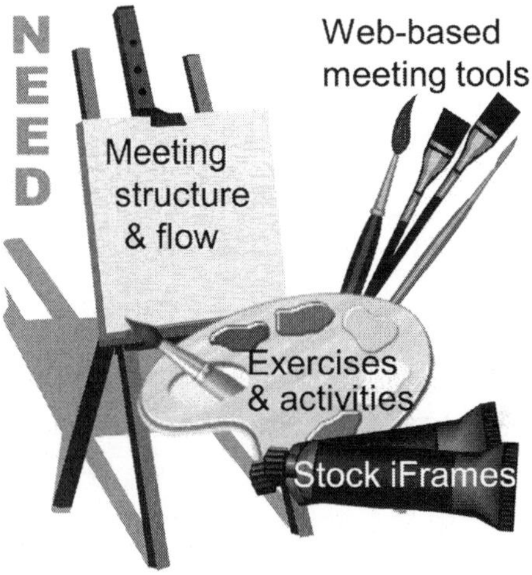

At some point you will be developing your own pigments and adapting them to achieve exactly the effects you want, but that takes a certain amount of practice, and in the meantime, you can find a ready-made source of such colours in Appendix 4 (we call them iFrames). In the spirit of developing your art, we would recommend that you browse that section of the book (which is actually in electronic form to provide easy access to the iFrames themselves, see page 211), reflect upon how and where you might use the iFrames, and begin to build them in wherever seems appropriate. To help you in this, the chart on the next page shows which standard iFrames can be utilised to support the various aims of meetings, introduced on page 37, and then built upon on page 77.

However, as you gain proficiency and confidence in utilising iFrames, remember that it is not only you to whom this world is novel, alien, and confusing, but in many cases your participants also. They will be used to (and comfortable with) physical rooms

Basic iFrame Selection Tool

Participative iFrames >

	iFrame Purpose		SWOT Diagram	Hopes & Concerns	Card Sort	6 Thinking Hats	Cause & Effect	Kipling List	Affinity Diagram	Creativity Tools	Matrix Diagram	Clothesline	Impact/Ease Grid	Forcefield	Planning Chart	Meeting Review
Q1 Needs	Understand situation	Align perspectives	✓	✓	✓	✓		✓	✓							
Q1 Needs	Explore issues	Develop insight	✓		✓	✓	✓	✓	✓	✓	✓			✓		
Q2 Plans	Generate solutions	Engage creativity			✓	✓			✓	✓	✓			✓		
Q2 Plans	Establish goals	Inspire aspirations			✓						✓	✓				
Q2 Plans	Agree strategy	Build commitment		✓	✓			✓	✓	✓	✓		✓	✓	✓	
Q3 Practice	Ensure teamwork	Develop relationships		✓							✓			✓		✓
Q3 Practice	Manage progress	Ensure responsibility	✓				✓			✓	✓			✓	✓	✓

with black and white canvases. If you make your 'art' too shocking they will struggle to engage with it at all. Initially you may need to consider:

- Limiting your use of iFrames to those that are more basic and easy to assimilate by participants
- Providing enhanced explanations and walkthroughs until people gain a real grasp of what they are doing
- Offering a short class in 'art appreciation' where participants can develop the skills and understanding they need prior to encountering the iFrames in your meetings.

Finally in our analogy, we come to the brushes; the tools we use to apply the pigment (events, exercises, activities) to the canvas (meeting needs and structure). These are the tools that are available on the Internet for hosting and controlling different aspects of your meeting, and for making the iFrames work in practice.[1] Typically, when we think of such tools we tend to restrict ourselves to the obvious meeting tools such as Live Meeting or WebEx, but these are just a small part of the available web-based meeting environment. Unlike physical meetings, the web-based meeting does not need to be constrained to a single forum at a single time, and can be several different things at once. Within a web-based meeting we can be in multiple places at the same time, and often are. In the past, this has been viewed as a problem, a source of distraction for people attending a web-based meeting, but embraced positively it is an opportunity to engage more of your people's thinking through a variety of channels.

As we indicated back on page 152, web-based technologies break through the paradigms of traditional meeting think, not just in the fact that we are limited by a physical geography, or in respect of the multi-channel think we have expounded so far, but further than that. The possibility of web-based technology gives us options to reconsider:

- Who is involved in the meeting, irrespective of location
- How much of the meeting they are involved in
- How much of them we are involving at that time (and whether there are other things that they can be doing in other windows/meetings at the same time)
- How many meetings we are involved in concurrently

[1] Some of these were covered at the end of the previous chapter, page 143.

- How much of the meeting is synchronous and how much of it happens asynchronously[1]
- What environment(s) we want for the meeting
- What a meeting actually is.

Much of this list may well remain fairly academic for you during your initial involvement with web-based meetings, and the main reason for its inclusion here is to illustrate that you may be less bound in your options than you might naturally assume.

The main web-based tools that you might wish to consider are:

- Scheduled meetings, which can be assembled with presentations, iFrames, and other tools ahead of time, and used in much the same way as you might consider a scheduled physical meeting
- Breakout rooms, which are a feature of some web-based meeting software, enable you to break people off to do different tasks and then review the result in plenary
- Ongoing meetings, which can also be assembled with presentations and iFrames, but provide the facility for people to enter the meeting at their convenience to review the current state of the content, and add in their own contributions
- Shared drawing software (such as GoogleDocs)[2], which can work in the same way as an ongoing meeting, and provides improved functionality for some iFrames. Fast refresh times

[1] 'Synchronous' simply means that we are all doing the same things at the same time (as in synchronised) and 'asynchronous' is the opposite – for instance off-line activities and actions.

[2] http://docs.google.com – but please see footnote 1 on next page.

mean that it can also be used in parallel with a scheduled meeting

- Online storage[1] (such as SharePoint), which can provide the facility for collaborative iFrames to be worked on by people offline, but usually not all together, and so they are limited in their support for a synchronous meeting
- A slight exception to this is OneNote on SharePoint, which works a bit like GoogleDocs draw but with greater functionality. Unfortunately the refresh time is at best eight seconds (currently over the web) and this can be a struggle in using it for synchronous work on collaborative iFrames
- Forums, which are a bit like a common structured email space where you can follow how ideas are evolving, and which can serve as a searchable repository of perspectives and resulting conclusions.

The most obvious place to start is the established web-meeting software, such as Live-Meeting or WebEx, but as you build confidence we would recommend exploring how you can integrate the other options.

Setting up the web-based meeting

The final step in implementing your design is to prepare the web-based tools for your meeting. Exactly how this is done is specific to each software vendor, and is therefore outside of the scope of this book. We have however developed some basic guidance on

[1] Depending on your corporate policy and firewall settings, you may need to work with your IT department to gain access to these and agree policies for what data will be used within online applications/storage and what will not.

how to access the information you need to do this. This can be found in Appendix 7.

On a more general note, virtually all the main web-based meeting software provides a fairly consistent set of functionality, which you can configure in different ways to meet the needs of your meeting. In summary the main elements are:

- The facility to load and manage a wide range of content, from presentations, video, text documents, whiteboards, and iFrames
- The facility to invite and organise participants, allow them permissions, and communicate with them to gain their views in a wide variety of ways
- The facility to pass control for programs and for annotation to different participants, to enable more collaborative involvement
- The facility to split the meeting up into smaller groups
- The facility to manage, record, and save the meeting and its outcomes in a number of different ways, including as an on-going project room.

Process mastery

The ongoing development of web-based meeting technology, the associated improvements in meeting design, and the resulting benefits for performance, people development, and culture hold the potential to transform organisations almost beyond recognition. The diagram on the next page (courtesy of iFacile.com) gives some sense of the influence and resulting impacts that are possible through enthusiastic and innovative adoption of this new potential.

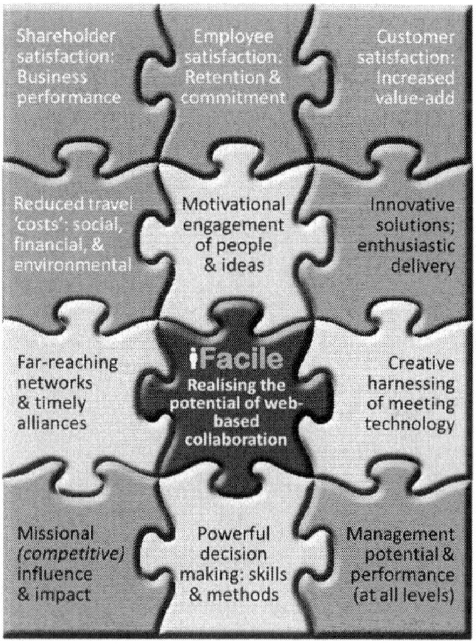

The approaches outlined in the preceding section will go a long way to helping people engage with these possibilities and develop core skills that will support them. But with the best will in the world, the artistic approach outlined above is barely more than 'dabbling' – inspired and energetic dabbling we hope, but it lacks the disciplines that are evident in true mastery of a skill. It lacks meta-process.

At some point, realisation of the full potential available will require you to utilise disciplines in the process of designing and facilitating your meetings – disciplines which with proficiency will be second nature, and almost subconscious, but disciplines nonetheless.

The most efficient and effective way to understand these disciplines, and to work with others to begin to master them, is through practical, experiential training. There are a lot of training courses available on web-based meetings, but please be aware that many of these may still be operating from an traditional meetings paradigm and therefore focus mainly on presentation, handling debate, and only the more basic aspects of participation such as polls, chat, and Q&A.

We recommend that you look for a training course which covers the following disciplines:

- Setting performance focused objectives for meetings
- Researching the start point of both situation and team
- Preparing participants for effective web-based meetings
- Selecting multi-channel processes/iFrames to achieve your objective
- Configuring these processes/iFrames into a meeting flow
- Using web-based tools to implement the flow
- Facilitation skills for web-based multi-channel meetings
- Evaluating meeting performance
- Addressing behavioural issues.

A list of current training providers can be found in Appendix 12. Alternatively, given the importance of this work, you might give some thought to developing your own training programme in-house.

One other advantage of a formal training programme, particularly one that is developed in-house, is that it brings some consistency to the forms of meetings being developed, and this familiarity with common techniques assists participants in making effective contributions from the outset.

However, apart from the time invested in training there is also clearly an investment to be made in preparation (which is what this chapter has been all about) and part of the issue here is that all of the preparation involved in meeting design takes time: from the offline discussions about how people see the purpose of the meeting, to the time spent structuring activities which will engage the creativity and experience of people; from the research into relevant articles and best practice to include as useful pre-reading, to harnessing the flow of the process to give the maximum opportunity to learning and insight. All of this needs time and space to do it properly.

However, a day's work by one individual in designing the meeting can pay back dividends in terms of the time saving of the increased efficiency of the meeting on everybody else's time. In many cases eight hours of investment by one manager can save ten other managers four hours each[1] and possibly a whole extra meeting. Of course that saving does not help the first manager directly, unless other managers start doing the same thing for the meetings that the first manager attends. Whether this works in practice depends on things we will cover in the next chapter.

In summary

As should always be the case in management, our first step is to define clearly what is needed to be done (to define the gap that the meeting is required to close). The second step is to clarify what sort of collaboration processes are required to fulfil that objective; whether a meeting is required at all and, if so, what sort of meeting.

Implementing the collaboration processes within the web-based meeting is actually a much easier task than implementing them in a physical meeting and there are a number of preformed guides and solutions to help you.

Developing your abilities in this area can be stepwise: doing something that you are confident in and then building upon it.

[1] Please refer back to sidebar on page 48.

This is a new area for many people, and so training will have a positive and cost-effective impact, and will help to build consistency of approach and establish a common standard of proficiency.

Outworking

Follow the steps in this chapter (page 161: Some practical steps in moving forward) to develop a few changes to your next web-based meeting, and then build upon these as you gain confidence.

Set yourself a target to gradually work through the iFrames that are available to support what you are trying to achieve in your meetings – see Appendix 4.

Use Appendices 8 and 9 to research your options for embracing process outside of the conventional meeting software.

Chapter 7

Addressing Organisational and Cultural Issues

In short

Management need to apply the same degree of measurement and control to the meetings process as they would to any other key business critical process in their organisation.

A story is told of the middle ages, when people were allowed to graze animals on common land. One piece of common land could support two animals per householder without risk of overgrazing. However, a few of the surrounding householders realised that they could easily put a third animal onto the common and increase their income. When others observed that people were doing this without sanction, they too chose to introduce further animals. Sadly, this meant that some of the existing animals were not getting the same amount of grazing as before, and so some of those who had previously adhered to the 'two animal policy' introduced third and fourth animals to adjust for the loss of fattening in the first two. Eventually the common became drastically overgrazed, and most of the animals died.

The story, known as 'The Tragedy of the Commons', is based on an essay written by Garrett Hardin to illustrate human behaviour around unregulated situations where individual gain may be at the cost of common good. It is a story which neatly highlights global issues around shared resources like fish stocks, pollution, etc.

It also illustrates management behaviour around meetings in most organisations. In the management situation, the limited resource is 'time' rather than 'grazing', and the 'animals' we place on this resource are events and activities which consume the time to deliver us outcomes (progress against our objectives). The 'tragedy' begins when we make choices which increase the efficiency of our use of time to the cost of the efficiency of others' use of time.

How do we do this in meetings? In practice there are a number of ways that this happens, and different organisations may have each to differing degrees:

- When people are late for the start of a meeting because something else is overrunning, do they: (a) reschedule what is overrunning and take the inefficiency hit on their own agenda; or (b) turn up late to the start of the meeting and pass the inefficiency hit on to others?
- When there is pre-reading to be done for a meeting, do people: (a) adjust their own schedules to make sure the pre-reading gets done; or (b) expect the meeting to fill in the gaps in the pre-reading even though it would repeat things for others who had been more diligent?
- When there is some one-on-one agreement to be reached in order to complete an action for the meeting, do people: (a) schedule time with the other person to finish things off so that the conclusion can be reported succinctly to the

meeting; or (b) take up everybody else's time in the meeting as bystanders to the final agreement?

- When spending two hours thinking about the design of a meeting could either make a two hour meeting of ten people either 10 per cent shorter, 10 per cent more effective, or both, do people: (a) find the time to invest in the design of the meeting; or (b) save the time in their own diaries and accept that the meeting may not be as efficient or effective as it could be?

The problem of the tragedy of the commons is that it is insidious. It begins with one or two people who gain personal efficiency from the (b)-behaviours listed above, and thereby deliver additional time pressures to everybody else. But if the behaviour of one or two individuals is not addressed, those time pressures cascade onto others, and they adopt the (b)-behaviours as a survival mechanism, and before long (b)-behaviours are the culture of the organisation, time becomes 'overgrazed' and everybody is overworked and stressed by the inefficiencies that result. The same behaviour is often evident in the forwarding of emails.

We raise this to stress the point that failing to take proper account of the cultural influences in how managers utilise time, and how they engage in meetings, has the potential to undermine any investment that you place in the other aspects you have read in these pages. And to be frank, we have good reason for concern. Many of the problems that currently exist in meeting performance, as reported in Chapter 2, arise precisely *because* the culture is *not* being properly managed from the top. And we do not mean posters setting out Value Statements stuck up around the building, or the monthly identification of a star employee.

So, what do we mean?

What does taking proper account of the cultural influences look like? In this chapter, we will explore six aspects to this question:

- What meeting behaviours do you actually need?
- How do you keep track of whether there is an issue with meeting performance and with the behaviours therein?
- How do you best prepare your people to influence the appropriate meeting behaviours on the ground?
- How do you create an environment which enables them to influence appropriate meeting behaviours effectively?
- How do you equip your people to facilitate that influence?
- How do you harvest the benefits?

Defining the meeting behaviours you need

The culture of the organisation *is* what happens in meetings. If meetings are customer focused, then the culture is customer focused. If meetings look for opportunities to develop people within what they are trying to achieve, then the culture of the organisation is to develop people. And conversely, whatever is not done in meetings is not the culture of the organisation.

If the intended culture is actively designed into meetings, then the resulting culture will be intentional, but if it is not, then whatever culture emerges will be intrinsic – a natural consequence of the interaction of the values of the people it employs. This is not necessarily a bad thing, but it means that you will not be in control of it beyond the point of recruitment.

Therefore, if your organisational culture is exactly where you want it to be, then you can be confident that whatever is naturally happening within your meetings is supportive of that culture. But if, as in most cases, you are seeking to influence the current culture of your organisation then you need to consider:

- What behaviours are currently valued within meetings in practice?
- How do these behaviours differ from those needed to support your intended vision?
- What needs to change within the meeting to stop rewarding 'wrong' behaviours (or allowing them to be rewarded) and start rewarding 'right' behaviours?

In respect of the phrase 'or allowing them to be rewarded', many of the rewards for 'bad' behaviours are inherent in the situation, and are not something we explicitly reward. For instance, the behaviours of poor preparation or lateness for the meeting are rewarded by the time saving achieved by the person who arrives poorly prepared or late. In fact we rarely actively reward 'bad' behaviours such as politics, or not-listening, etc., we just fail to redress the rewards that are inherent within them.

If we want to change the culture of our organisation, we need to start with what happens in our meetings. In terms of meeting design, this requires that we think about how our meeting is to positively influence the culture of the organisation at the same time as defining our objectives for it.

The transition to greater use of web-based meetings represents the best opportunity organisations have ever had to address and manage the culture of their organisations, but this will not happen by accident. For it to happen effectively it must be entirely intentional, and it must begin with a clear 'visionary' definition of what is to be achieved through this transition. And that vision needs to be clear, compelling, and sufficiently valuable to the organisation's future that senior management will see driving progress toward that vision as a true priority for their time and decisions.

To help you with this, we have used our analysis of the survey data to draft a vanilla definition of a generic vision[1] for the adoption of multi-channel meetings through web-based technology, and you are welcome to use this as a base for adding in your own flavour of what you want to see achieved.

However, we do strongly recommend that it is only a base. For it to be effective, it needs to be owned by the senior management team, and that requires that they engage with it intellectually and emotionally as a key step to what they want to achieve within the organisation. It needs to be something of sufficient import to them, that monitoring progress against it is top of their agenda, and that they are willing to go through a degree of personal discomfort to make it happen.

And there will be some degree of personal discomfort, because most of the senior team probably got to their position through

[1] This can be found in Appendix 6.

their proficiency in the old culture of meetings – their meeting habits will have become hardened through years of positive reinforcement, and reaction under stress. And we are asking them to give all of this up – for what?

The adoption of the ideas in this book has tremendous potential, but unless that is translated into a *for what* for your organisation, and your senior team are willing to sacrifice aspects of their own behaviour and responses, then frankly it is not going to happen. The 'tremendous potential' needs to be translated into a clear vision, your own vision, for the impact on the performance and future of your organisation. And then you must take responsibility for making sure it is happening.

Keeping track of meeting performance

The key first step in this is to equip yourselves with the regular accurate data that is currently so absent in many organisations – data concerning the achievement, impact, and quality of meetings. Within the web-based environment, generating the data is relatively easy,[1] but the cultural change will be to invest time in collating, reviewing, and responding to it from the senior levels of the organisation.

The senior team needs to invest time on a monthly basis:

- Reviewing data on what is actually happening in meetings and how this is trending over time, and comparing this against their vision for the impact of these meetings

[1] Simple survey tools can easily be appended to web-based meetings. For more information on this, please see Appendix 14.

- Understanding the root causes behind any drops in trend and deficits in the intended performance
- Engaging in honest and frank discussions amongst themselves regarding the extent to which they, and their ways of working, may need to change to address these root causes and act as a vanguard
- Setting out programmes of practical measures to correct remaining issues and to ensure their progress in doing so.

From the perspective that has commonly been taken toward web-based meetings to date, such a serious level of focus may seem a bit over the top. But, from the perspective of the role that meetings play within your organisation, in terms of management time consumption, the efficacy of that time, the impact on leadership and culture, the linkage (or lack of) to driving performance, and to the development of talent, this level of focus becomes both expected and essential. Meetings are *the* key lever by which you will 'engage more of the practical creativity and resourcefulness of your people in bringing about a step change in performance'. How much is it worth to you to get it right?

The pivotal element of this step is the metrics that will be used to collate and analyse meeting performance. Some of these will be specific to your vision, but others are likely to be more generic, and reflect the individual and collective judgement of the people attending the meeting in respect of a number of the following:

- Proportion of required pre-work (including pre-reading) completed for the meeting
- Existence of defined objectives which relate to the performance goals and/or vision of the organisation

- Appropriateness of meeting process/agenda to deliver that objective
- Perceived efficiency of the meeting in delivering the objective
- Incidence of behaviours which delayed progress, marred commitment, or were contrary to the organisation's values
- Proportion of issues concerning behaviour that were addressed during or after the meeting
- Perceived levels of belief in the accuracy of the conclusions and people's commitment to them.

There is a paradigm shift required here. In any other process within your organisation, these metrics would be inevitable, but somehow we in the West tend to think that 'management is above all of that', and that they should be accorded the honour and trust to be exempt from such checks. But many of the operating processes which originally benefitted from these disciplines have now migrated from our shores, and more of our resources and hopes are now invested in work that would traditionally be seen as a 'white-collar' role. In other words, the nature of 'work' has moved up a level in the West, and the evidence is that we are not doing too well at this in process terms. Monitoring our effectiveness in these management processes as a means to identifying issues and focusing on addressing them does not of itself reflect a loss of 'honour and trust'. If we use the metrics to work with people to gain insight into and understand their difficulties, and then work in partnership with them to resolve these difficulties, then we reflect honour and trust in them as a valuable person worthy of investment. Alternatively, if we ignore the frustrations that people clearly experience in meetings, then where is the honour and trust in that?

The list of bullet points on the previous page may be collected at once; or there may be 'phased' work to identify and address areas for improvement. But it should be noted that the use of web-based technology makes gathering and analysing such data relatively easy, and its collection emphasises the importance the organisation now places on the things that we are measuring. 'Meetings' represent the process by which the aspirations of shareholders (or stakeholders) are deployed into the actions of an organisation's people. And yet, as a process, it is neither measured nor controlled by those who have most need for assuring its effectiveness and efficiency. The future success of web-based meetings both *requires* and *enables* that to change.

But web-based meetings are only part of the meeting framework, and our expectation is to use web-based meetings as a nursery for practice within physical meetings. And here the nature of measurement is not quite so straightforward. However, it is every bit as vital, and there is no reason why the survey tools developed to measure web-based meetings should not be extended to physical meetings, and no reason not to expect managers to collate and respond to their own performance in this regard.

Preparing your people

Given the importance of meetings to the operation and decision making within an organisation, it is surprising how little training takes place to prepare people for their part within them. It seems to be taken for granted that even the most junior employee and the freshest recruit will intuitively understand the part they need to play within the meeting. Furthermore, beyond short courses on presentation skills, and some rudimentary guidance on setting an agenda, many people who set up and run meetings have never had any formal training in how to do so.

This same mind-set appears to have been carried over to the world of web-based meetings. To date, many organisations have simply adopted the available products and provided very little in the way of training or development in their use.[1]

But anybody who has an eye to see and an ear to hear should be aware that all is not right in this. Issues with the way physical meetings work are evident to all who have paused to consider the fact – the results of Chapter 2 are just a collation of those considerations. It is equally obvious to those who have involvement in web-based meetings that there is much to take issue with both in terms of their own understanding of the tool, and in the realisation of web-based meetings in practice.

We really do stand on the edge of a huge increase in potential, but we cannot assume that we can grasp this potential effectively simply with native wit and common sense. Learning by trial and error in this field is simply neither efficient nor sufficient to achieve the full potential available, and organisations that fail to realise this fact will suffer the consequences.

---

[1] 64 per cent of people running web-based meetings have received no formal training, 95 per cent of people feel that there is a significant amount of training that they still need. Survey data – see Appendix 2, reference point V.

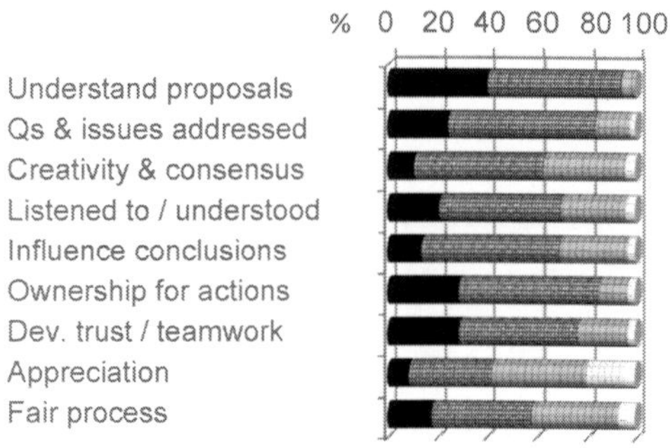

If we are to realise the benefits that are available to us in this area, we need to invest in developing the proficiency of our people to utilise the technical functionality that is available, and to configure it into an effective process for carrying the thinking and commitment of their people forward. The business case for doing so is more than justifiable on travel savings alone in most cases.

But it is not only the people who will be facilitating web-based meetings that will benefit from training. The diagram on the right shows the weight that people attach to various objectives for their participation in meetings. Part of the delivery of this can be achieved by the facilitator's choice of iFrames and tools, but not all of it. The remainder needs to come from the participant, and this requires a certain base level of proficiency in those participants. Further-more, multi-channel meetings and web-based tools will be alien to many people, and sadly, different levels of understanding in participants and confusion over how to perform simple tasks can make early meetings inefficient as people try to cope with new approaches, or wait for other people to catch up. It takes less than a day to prepare someone for attending their first participative web-based meeting, and it can save a lot more than that in avoiding inefficiency and confusion.

Training participants for web-based meetings also allows a stake to be set in the ground about meeting behaviours; to mark this as the point where we begin to leave behind some of the attitudes which cost us so dearly in terms of our current physical meetings. And perhaps, when we have learned what makes our web-based meetings successful, and imported it back into physical meetings, we may need to provide training on this also.

But for behaviours to change sustainably, we cannot rely on training alone.

Creating a supportive environment

How will a facilitator respond to someone who prevents progress in a meeting because they habitually fail to complete their actions, or who creates inefficiency because they regularly fail to prepare appropriately? And how will they respond to someone who diminishes buy-in in others by ignoring the ground rules, and dominating the meeting, particularly when it is a senior or valued member of staff? And how will you support them in what they do?

Your answers to these questions will either reduce the incidence of these behaviours, and thereby progress the benefits of effective meetings, or they will maintain the status quo and undermine your hopes and expectations.

Nadler and Lawler once wrote an excellent paper on motivation,[1] full of insightful research and clear logic, and at the end of the paper, they summed the whole of it up in just one sentence: 'Organisations usually get what they reward, not what they want'. The truth is that, at some level, each organisation functions as an

[1] *Motivation: a diagnostic approach*, Nadler and Lawler, 1977.

economy, and within that economy there are natural costs and paybacks.

We are aware of this when we offer bonuses, rewards, and other incentives – when we do this we recognise that the intrinsic payback to the individual does not justify the cost that they have to put in, and so we augment it with something 'additional'. Similarly, we introduce rules and penalties to discourage people from taking decisions that give them payback at the cost to others and to the organisation, though most of these tend to be quite severe and are therefore only exceptionally applied.

Where we struggle, and where Nadler and Lawler's closing point is most apposite, is those behaviours that are too trivial for the level of penalties that we have, but which nonetheless benefit the person doing the behaviour at a cost to their colleagues and the organisation as a whole. Viewed through Nadler and Lawler's pithy observation we can see that although we might look negatively on such behaviours – such as departmental politics, delaying actions, etc. – the 'organisation' (the system, the environment, the way things are) inherently rewards it, and so it happens. And it happens most in, and around, meetings.

To overcome this unintentional reward system, you will really seriously need to consider the questions posed in the first paragraph of this section (page 187), and reach your own conclusions about what you need to do. But you might like to consider the approach outlined in the sidebar on the facing page.

While executive teams may be naturally reluctant to take strong steps in this area, the sad alternative is clearly spelled out in

Sidebar: Managing meeting behaviour

- Use your vision of meeting benefits and behaviours to define a clear and explicit code of conduct, and a scale of skills which reflect proficiency in that conduct
- Ensure that this code of conduct and scale of skills is clearly part of delivering training on web-based meetings, and that your senior team model it themselves in all meetings
- Make assessment against the code a required part of the appraisal system, and include proficiency against the scale of skills within objective setting for all people involved in meetings
- Ensure that all line managers seek formal assessments from facilitators regarding the performance of their people in their projects and meetings, and that the participants know that their facilitator will be required to submit this feedback
- Ensure rewards to those who are actively growing in their ability and disposition to ensure meetings are effective; actively, explicitly, and determinedly withhold rewards (e.g., promotions, pay-rises, bonuses) from those who are not
- Monitor the effectiveness of your strategy through your meeting metrics.

Nadler and Lawler's closing sentence. At the moment it is all too evident that most organisations experience counterproductive behaviours that generate the results we saw in Chapter 2. It is also clear that the inherent nature of organisations rewards these. Unless we change this, the behaviours will adapt and continue, and the consequences will be felt in the performance of our organisations.

However, on a brighter note, as long as you have good metrics to give you accurate feedback on what is really happening in, and emerging from, your meetings, you will only need to do this to the degree that you need to make progress, and you will be able to see what level that is through your data.

Equipping your people to facilitate

Unlike large format video conferencing and Telepresence, most people already have on their desk what they need to take part in a web-based meeting. However, there are a number of small investments[1] which could make people's involvement, and particularly their role in facilitation, both easier and more effective.

The first of these is to set up their PC with two screens. Facilitating a multi-channel meeting over the web can involve a lot of windows open on the desktop: two meeting windows, separate windows for the back-channels such as chat and meeting notes, windows to shared documents in SharePoint, browser windows to something like GoogleDocs, windows displaying part-

[1] The likely total cost for the hardware investments described on the following page is likely to be in the order of £200 to £400 per head. Reference PCWorld pricelists 2011.

icipant status and content management, etc. The provision of a second screen makes a huge difference in being able to organise and keep an overview of all of these windows. All that may be required is a second monitor[1] and perhaps a second (or dual screen) video card – all of the software for it is already included in most releases of Windows.

The next area of investment is a good headset with microphone. These may need to work with both the telephone system and the computer, depending on which audio options are employed in the web-based meeting. The use of a headset is essential for an open office environment in order to screen out office noise and avoid disturbing other colleagues in the office, but it is also useful within an office to avoid feedback, improve sound quality both ways, and also to provide a visual cue to people wandering past that you are engaged in a meeting and therefore not open to being interrupted unless it is important.

A third good investment is a reasonable quality webcam. This may seem a surprising choice if you interpret earlier statements in the book as a denigration of video. We are not in any way against video – we see it as a very useful addition, and we look forward to a time when Internet bandwidth is sufficient to see the faces of the people who are listening rather than the people who are talking. Our reservations stem only from the fact that, while video is valuable, it is not so valuable that it is worth sacrificing the other functionality and convenience of web-based meetings to

[1] Users who have a laptop with a docking station and a desktop monitor (which is commonly the case) already have two screens. All that may be required in this situation is to reconfigure the settings to extend the desktop across both screens. This is a very easy thing to do, but you may need some help from IT support to talk you through it the first time around.

obtain (as in the case – currently at least – of Telepresence and video conferencing). A summary of the hardware needs for web-based meetings is included in Appendix 10.

And this brings us onto the software needs. We would encourage you to invest in a web-meeting software licence which includes as much as possible of the functionality outlined in Chapter 5, page 143 onwards. For many organisations, particularly the larger ones, you will probably already have done so as part of your IT licence package. In respect of other relevant supporting software, there are a number of packages that we would encourage you to consider, and we have included these as Appendix 9.

And, on the subject of software, you will almost certainly need to engage your IT department in your vision so that they can make the necessary provisions in terms of licenses, bandwidth and firewalls – they would be best placed to advise on what is required in this area.

It may seem strange to be so specific about the technology required, but it is very easy to underestimate the role of equipment limitations on facilitating or participating in web-based meetings, and the consequences can impact the whole meeting. Conversely, if people can rely on their equipment they will feel significantly more comfortable and confident in their participation.

All in all, the investments required in hardware and software are trivial – approximately 1–2 per cent of the expected annual travel saving. The biggest investment required is in appropriate training of your people to get the best use out of the technology. The biggest investment that is likely to be made is in *not* training your people.[1]

Harvesting the benefits

Providing your vision and metrics are clearly set out, harvesting the benefits should be a natural consequence of your work. But these may only be the obvious benefits. There are other potential benefits which may be not so obvious.

As your organisation and its people grow in their proficiency in web-based meetings, there may be opportunities for harnessing this capability in other ways. Things you might consider include:

- Allowing a greater use of home-working, or participation through remote sites or serviced office space
- Enabling greater flexibility in working hours
- Saving on the floor area required for established offices
- Engaging more part-time staff and portfolio workers, or even stay-at-home parents
- Retaining staff who you might otherwise lose as their family situation changes
- Engaging staff from countries where the relevant skills and/or networks may be better or more economical.

[1] 'If you think training is expensive, try ignorance', quote attributed to Peter Drucker.

In summary

A lot of the current performance issues reported in Chapter 2 exist because those at senior levels fail to take effective responsibility for managing meeting performance. The consequences of this are a major barrier to creativity, engagement and step changes in performance.

Sustained achievement of the benefits outlined in this book are dependent on management facing up to this responsibility through values, metrics, training, and resources.

While this may be initially targeted at web-based meetings, it also needs to support the migration of the learning back into physical meetings as this becomes appropriate.

Outworking

Establish metrics to understand the quality of meetings across your own area of responsibility.

Set a clear vision for the difference you want to achieve through better meetings and measure progress toward it.

Implement the messaging, metrics, training, and technical support required to achieve your vision.

Chapter 8

Extending the Approach into Physical Meetings

In short

In order to import the multi-channel approach successfully back into physical meetings, changes will need to take place in the facilities, culture and thinking of the organisation.

As you come to this chapter, there is every possibility that you have been inspired to change the way meetings are conducted in your organisation, but wish to take a more direct route than the web-based meeting 'skunk-works'[1] approach. This chapter is written primarily from the perspective of transferring back into physical meetings what you have learned about multi-channel approaches in web-based meetings; the advice contained within its pages will provide guidance to help you do just that. But, unless you are the chief executive of a relatively small organisation, in which you have direct influence over your organisation's meetings, and possibly less cause to use web-based meetings, you would be best advised not to do this.

---

[1] Skunk-works is a term which refers to an environment where the normal rules and ways of working have been suspended and replaced with whatever accelerates development and R&D. It is a term which originated with Lockheed.

There are two main arguments for this:

1. The proven resilience of the physical meeting environment: As a consultant, the author has spent the last 25 years introducing different aspects of strategy and culture change within large organisations, always with enough success to achieve the organisation's immediate goals, usually over a period of a number of years. But it has always involved a lot of work and a lot of time; continuously pushing against a tide of established practice, mindsets, and lethargy. It is hard work (more so for the client than for the consultant) and it is easy to see things slowly drifting back over time as the focus moves onto other things. We must not underestimate the resilience of traditions, custom, and practice; of drifting back to things that feel as familiar as a well-worn pair of shoes, and this is especially true of interpersonal behaviours in general and meeting practice in particular. How many large organisations have tried to introduce better meeting practices in the past, through approaches like Total Quality, or direct training in setting agendas and meeting behaviour codes? And how long was it before things eventually began to drift back toward how they were, possibly under the weight of years of tradition and practice (and even upbringing)? When it began its slow, inexorable drift, did the managers recognise it, and did they have the personal bandwidth to address the slide, or was their time and focus already invested in other hugely important things?

If you run a small organisation, any risk of drift within it is far more obvious, and your scope of direct influence is far better placed to respond economically and effectively. But if you run a larger organisation, we would commend you to pilot the approach within web-based meetings first for all of the reasons outlined in Chapter 5. Doing so means that you will have far more people who are champions of the approach, at all levels of the organisation, who are deeply rooted in the practice and benefits, and who will resist the drift on your behalf. Establishing the practices in web-based meetings will provide a living anchor for the practices you want to introduce and sustain in *all* of your meetings.

2. The growing potential of the web-based environment.

Consider the following:

- Physical meeting spaces are expensive, and because of their limited supply usually require booking in advance, thus they are not always available when your people can most conveniently use them. It is also rare to book them for a very short meeting because 'getting there', and 'waiting for others to arrive' can involve more time than the meeting itself. Dedicated physical project rooms are even more of a luxury
- Permanently allocated desk space is expensive, and people often work more efficiently at home. Home working also provides access to a wider labour market than fixed office hours, but incurs greater costs if attending physical meetings
- The trade in intermediate goods and services is growing all the time, and so is the potential to find good partners to help you in your work, but organising physical meetings to build the level of relationship you need to make the alliance work at its best is likely to prove costly, and therefore not involve all of the staff you would ideally like to include
- The same is true of other physical meetings with customers, suppliers and other organisations; they carry significant over-

head in time and cost, and therefore mean that they are not as brief or as frequent as might be optimum for you
- You are working in a world where people's proficiency and affinity for the web is growing all the time, and where weakness in this area may place your organisation at a disadvantage.

In other words, there may be real advantages for you to engage with web-based meetings even if you do not appear to have any immediate necessity for them, and therefore it may benefit you to reconsider whether there is actually a case for you to begin developing these meeting practices within the web-based environment after all.

Whichever route you decide to take, in this chapter we look at how the practices laid out in the last three chapters can be applied (and/or applied back) into your physical meetings:

- How meeting facilities can be developed to accommodate more participative practices in meetings
- How to translate the meeting design elements of Chapter 6 into the physical environment
- The role of leadership in breaking down some of the existing paradigms and practices in physical meetings, and in introducing new ones
- How the cultural elements introduced in Chapter 7 can be extended over physical meetings
- How to incorporate some of the technological advantages from the web-based environment into physical meetings.

Meeting facilities

What thoughts come to mind when you look at the photograph on the right? It looks modern, relaxed, inviting, attractive; perhaps you feel that it looks a good place to hold a meeting, and that you might like to carry over the feel of it into your own meeting rooms? Perhaps your own meeting rooms already look quite similar to this? But what sort of meeting would be held in such a meeting room? To what extent does it encourage the adoption of best-practice meeting processes, participation, and multi-channel inputs; or to what extent does it actually reinforce an antiquated model of meetings that has remain unchanged over centuries?

This next picture may help you to answer this question. It is of a painting made in 1604, of a meeting held over 400 years ago. Does the layout look somewhat familiar? It certainly adds new meaning to the phrase: 'We have got to stop meeting like this!'

The board room style of meeting harks back to the feudal control structures of the Middle Ages, when the focus was very much one of direction rather than participation. Even the language used arises from that period of history – the 'board' being a large plank set up on trestles, and the 'chairman' being the important person sat in the chair at the end nearest to the warmth of the hearth and furthest from the draught of the door.

But the levels of participation that we have set our sights on require a different set up; one in which everybody gets a chance to contribute evenly, where ideas can be represented visually, refined, combined, and brought together into a shared conclusion. It is entirely possible to do this in a physical meeting, as off-site workshops can demonstrate, but not one in which everybody is stuck in seats around a large table. Practical participation requires the ability to move around unhindered; it needs easy access to large spaces where the range of contributions are held, worked-on, and pulled together (usually on the walls); it needs energy and movement and flow; it needs space that can be quickly adapted to what best supports the design of the meeting and the processes being employed.

Step one in applying the lessons of this book to physical meetings is a matter of ensuring your meeting rooms do not constrain your meetings to working around a table. This tends to require small, easily moved, modular tables rather than a large fixed arrangement, and for the furniture to occupy no more than half the room size in either dimension. It may not look as impressive as boardroom mahogany, but if you are relying so much on imposing visual impact to influence the outcomes it is not difficult to see why you might have a vestigial sympathy for feudal practices.

It also requires that the wall spaces are large and uncluttered, and able to support people working on large templates (the physical equivalent of iFrames) without tripping over each other. This is best facilitated by an absence of wall fittings and fixed pictures, and by ensuring that key equipment such as sockets, switches, controls, safety instructions, and fire alarms are grouped in places where they do not disrupt an otherwise large expanse of plain wall. It is also important to ensure that the walls are tolerant to temporary adhesives such as sticky tack and sticky notes. While a number of rooms do now have a rail just below the ceiling which serves to clip flipcharts into place, the reality is that this rail is often not sufficiently flexible or reliable to cope with the full range of interactive displays you will wish to use. Magnetic walls are somewhat more reliable and flexible, but you tend to need a shed-load of magnets, and they often go missing. Statically charged polypropylene sheets (plastic film whiteboards) work very well but, despite being relatively inexpensive, their cost can add up and present a bit of an obstacle.

Beyond that, you also need some way of capturing the outputs (high-resolution camera) and some way of presenting them back (ceiling mounted video projector, and screen).

Of course, if you really want to push the boat out you could introduce totally technology enabled walls to your meeting room (see the section on introducing technology into physical meetings at the end of this chapter).

Meeting design

Key to bringing the learning on meeting design (Chapter 6) into physical meetings is ensuring that all those people who are running physical meetings have had their paradigms on meetings shifted, and fully appreciate their importance, purpose, and the need for process within them. Where they have come to these meetings through the web-based meetings approach, this should already be established, but it is likely to prove more of an issue with those who have not, and they will probably require some level of training to build the necessary insight and ownership, not least in terms of the difference between Tag and Tackle Meetings and the importance of participation in the latter.

Having established ownership for the idea of meetings as a process, it is then important that the people who are designing these meeting processes appreciate the range of tools that are available to support them. Virtually all of the iFrames which work in web-based meetings have counterparts in physical meetings. These are in part explained on page 102, but there are also a number of excellent books on the subject.[1] However, the overall picture may be a little daunting at first, and it may be useful to reconsider the stepwise approach explained in Chapter 6 (page 161: 'Some practical steps in moving forward'); although this has been written from the perspective of web-based meetings, it is also applicable to physical meetings.

Finally, it is vital that people appreciate the importance of investing preparation time in meeting design. Those who come to these physical meetings through the web-based route will have initially received the argument as a cost saving over their travel time, and then subsequently seen the dividends of their investment in what emerged from the meeting. But for those who come directly into applying this to physical meetings, we must not underestimate

[1] A list of further reading can be found in Appendix 15.

the obstacle that this investment represents, particularly in the absence of any immediate pay-off. The temptation to short-change it will be significant, and you will need to put a lot of effort into selling the benefits and making sure that it happens.

The role of leadership

A lot has been said in Chapter 3 on the role of leadership, and how it needs to focus on the mechanisms of reception rather than those of transmission (page 77), but this is not an easy thing to accept. It takes a large amount of faith to let go of more directive techniques in the belief that more participative techniques will bring you through to a good or even better place, and that is true even when you are skilled in using the participative techniques. In other words, you will need to train those who are to exercise this form of participative management in the techniques they need to use, and to build their proficiency and their confidence to use them effectively. The alternative is that they will not see the results they need, and they will revert under any form of stress, and the participative approach will not be maintained.

But furthermore, even for those who have been through the web-based meeting route, the skills of facilitation for a physical meeting are actually subtly different to those for a virtual meeting, and will require a degree of adaptation. Once again, training will prove helpful here, but only in the techniques, since the core understanding will already be in place. A list of facilitation interventions for both physical and web-based meetings can be found in Appendix 11.

Ensuring an effective meeting culture

Those organisations who are adapting from their success in implementing the web-based meeting approach are likely to find that many of their cultural structures, established out of the learning from Chapter 7, will serve almost equally well in physical meetings. They will have established top-level support for the way meetings should take place, delivered relevant training, set out and demonstrated their values, and recorded progress against their vision for all of this, addressing any shortfalls within that. The only real issue will be in migrating their metrics for meeting performance across to the physical environment, but if they are willing to utilise web-based survey tools as an integral part of their physical meeting arrangements, even that will not prove too onerous.

However, those organisations planning to implement the ideas in this book directly into physical meetings will need to implement the necessary cultural support from scratch (and it is all 'necessary'). But their workload in this regard is likely to be no more onerous that it would be to establish the same culture for web-based meetings, and much of the guidance contained in Chapter 7 applies to both. The only area which will prove more of a struggle is in establishing effective metrics, but persevering with this struggle is crucial, for above all else, the absence of metrics for the performance of meetings has probably been the biggest single factor in how they have remained so bad for so long.

Introducing technology into physical meetings

I have long had a dream, which I hope to bring to fulfilment at some point, of a large octagonal room built up from 16 pen-enabled panels, backlit from 16 short-throw projectors, each of which is linked to a separate instance of an interactive visual package such as Google-docs draw or OneNote, and where the contributions made on every wall can be brought together and moved around, and put back where they were in the blink of an eye. People contribute to what is around them either directly on the wall or via tablets of some kind, or even via their position or movement over an interactive floor; and drop down screens enable the group to work as easily in syndicates or plenary.

Now that may be way too far off the radar for most organisations, but even so, the quality and reliability of hardware, software, and web-based options can significantly enhance the quality and efficiency of setting-up, managing, and reporting a participative physical meeting, and with far less investment than the ideas proposed in the previous paragraph. Some aspects of this are already common place, such as the use of SharePoint or its equivalents for undertaking and sharing preparation on documents before the meeting. But others can include the use of voting tools or affinity diagrams from people's laptops within the meeting, and displayed on the projector screen, or the use of web-based survey tools to record feedback on the meeting performance (as mentioned earlier).

Conversely, the more costly and involved a central meeting facility becomes, the more difficult it becomes to access. The future of collaboration will move to an 'always-connected' world and, within those connections, the West will rediscover its competitive position in the world, and so we need to be wary of changes and developments which make better interactions possible for the few rather than for the many.

In summary

It is possible to apply the lessons in this book directly into physical meetings, but it will prove significantly easier to pilot new meeting approaches in web-based meetings and then import the learning back into physical meetings.

To support participation, physical meeting rooms will need lots of space, clear walls, and easily moved modular furniture.

Education is needed to break down long-held physical meeting habits and reinforce the need for participation.

Meeting performance metrics will need to be introduced/extended into physical meetings, and issues in performance addressed.

There is real scope to adopt some of the underlying web-based technology to enhance and support physical meetings.

Outworking

Establish metrics of performance for physical meetings and monitor them.

Ensure your meeting rooms are set up to encourage and enable participation.

Make adjustments to your culture to ensure effective growth in your meeting performance.

Conclusion

We began this book with an adaptation of a biblical meeting, indifferentiable from any modern meeting in terms of its form and process. In its original form, the meeting was concerned with whether people had to conform to Jewish laws and traditions before they could be allowed to receive the Holy Spirit. And perhaps that is a good place to end as well.

This historic meeting from AD *c.*50, later to be known as the Council of Jerusalem, paved a way for literally hundreds of millions of believers (including the Author) to pursue their faith. It cut through the key obstacles to what was really important and then considered what additionally needed to be done in order to make what was important sustainable.

While web-based meetings are trivial in comparison, there are still some pale echoes of that great meeting in the opportunities that now face us:

- We too have a hope that people in our organisations can be more fully engaged and inspired in working out their (and our) destiny
- We too are faced with expected practices and traditions which trace back through millennia, and which act as a practical barrier to us

- We too have a decision to make on which might hang the (working) lives of many people, both currently and into the future.

We hope that in the pages of this book we have done justice to the roles that Paul and Barnabus (Paul and Barni) would have played in this crucial decision. It is your own council that will deliver *that* judgement.

But before you rush on to close this book, please pause for a moment and reflect on what we are really talking about here. The process we have been talking about in the last eight chapters consumes 2/3 of your management time. It is a major factor in your future business success. It is the key mechanism for engaging the ideas and commitment of your people. And it is not working well. How big a priority should this be for you?

The word 'meeting' and our association of it with a universal, commonplace, routine distracts us from this reality. Every psychological link we have with that word draws us to demote it to the mundane, and calls us to move on past it to something important and exciting.

Do you not sense that?

And does it not alarm you that there must be something terribly wrong here in the organisational psyche? How can we take such a crucial process for granted, demoting it to a ubiquitous and unquestioned commodity by which we address other things?

Winston Churchill said, 'Men occasionally stumble over the truth, but most of them pick themselves up and hurry off as if nothing ever happened.'

Now, here, at this point in the book, you too have stumbled over the truth. What you do next could make a huge different to your working life, and to the working lives of those around you.

The takeaway

The call to arms is simply this:

1. Take responsibility for developing accurate metrics for *your*[1] meeting performance, which reflect the extent to which they really engage the qualities of your people (e.g., creativity, commitment). Report them regularly at executive level

2. Research the extent to which you are using the full potential of web-functionality to establish web-based meetings as an effective alternative to travel (or even as an alternative to co-location)

3. Use the functionality of web-based meetings to measure and refine their effectiveness, and to initiate changes within the organisational culture which will drive and maintain meeting effectiveness in your area

4. Import your learning back into physical meetings as you develop confidence in your strategies.

Use this book and its web-based appendices to help you to do these things, however big or small your organisation, and whatever

[1] The performance of meetings (physical and virtual) within your scope of influence and authority.

level of management you are within it. You may not have the control and authority to do all that you want, but in all probability (and with sufficient determination) you have enough control and authority to do more than is happening currently. It is a myth to believe that change always begins at the top of an organisation; change begins wherever it can take hold of the heart and the imagination of someone who is brave enough to make a stand. What happens at the top simply makes that an easier and more obvious thing to do.

Web-based meetings are nothing short of a watershed; a point at which organisations will either grasp the branch that is being held out to them and pull their meeting processes out of the dark ages, or where they will continue to be borne along in the stream, never really in control of what is happening (or how it happens) in the murky depths beneath them. Far from being 'simply an alternative to travel', they represent an easy, expedient, and cost-effective first step toward a process which supports and sustains all that is best in management and leadership thinking. And it is a step which can be taken well, or a step on which we can all too easily miss our footing.

Our hope, in the pages of this book, is that we may have been able to shine a light on where best to place your foot, and how you might begin to shift your weight upon it. But, as always, the first step is undeniably yours. We hope you take it, we hope you take it soon, and we hope you take it well.

Appendices

In a field where technology advances almost daily, appendices risk being out of date within months of being written. To address this issue we have taken a dose of our own medicine and stored them online. This enables us to keep them updated, to equip you with downloadable content, which can be edited within your own systems, and to provide hyperlinks to other useful material. It also enables you to add in your own ideas and comments.

To access them go to www.meetingbydesign.org/appendix and then type the password MBDAPP into the page which opens.

Appendix 1: Key findings from Meetings Survey

Appendix 2: Key findings from Travel and Web-Meetings Survey

Appendix 3: Survey guidance for reviewing your organisation

Appendix 4: Basic iFrames for multi-channel work in web-based meetings

Appendix 5: Steps to practical implementations of the conclusions

Appendix 6: A generic vision for the transition of greater use of web-based meetings

Appendix 7: Using software for web-based collaboration – getting started

Appendix 8: Web-based developments that support Tag Meetings

Appendix 9: Other relevant supporting software

Appendix 10: Relevant supporting hardware

Appendix 11: Facilitation interventions for physical and virtual meetings

Appendix 12: Available training courses

Appendix 13: Useful links

Appendix 14: Meeting review tools

Appendix 15: Further reading

Acknowledgements

This book would not have been possible without the support of many people, not least those who we cajoled in their efforts with the promise of notoriety and the eternal recognition of their names enshrined on these pages. My heartfelt thanks go to: Albert Binns, Alison Evans, Andreas Edler, Andrew Boulton, Andrew Cleaves, Andrew Jackson, Andrew Peters, Andrew Roberts, Andrew Taylor, Andy Haasz, Andy Pilling, Angus Bain, Arthur Taylor, Ashton Hunt, Benj Street, Bharat Popat, Bill Pigg, Brian Batchelor, Brian Holliday, Carl Saxby, Chris Tattersall, Chris Zanetti, Christina Davey, Clare Holden, Costa Fafalios, Daniel Jones, Dave Brokish, Dave Pickles, David Houldridge, David Newey, David Owen, David Winder, Dean Heimbigner, Dennis Ciborowski, Derek Maidlow, Derek Silcock, Diana Brown, Diane Hancock, Dietmar Harteveld, Dilip Popat, Dorothy McCulloch, Emma Bush, Eric Rettig, Gene Edmiston, Guan Aik, Gwyneth Scolari, Helen Cole, Ian Errington, Ian Harteveld, Ian May, Jacqui Zanetti, Jamie MacAlister, Janet Lange, John Davies, John Dowden, Jonathan Chappel, Judie Davies, Judith Wainwright, Juergen Maier, Karen Jackson, Kath Russell, Kevin Downes, Kevin Thompson, Klaus Gotthardt, Klaus Hofmann, Len Geddes, Len Pendle, Leo van den Heuvel, Lilian Chu, Linda Cook, Lizi Jenkins, Lorna McInroy, Luke Shave, Malcolm Denham, Marc Das, Marion Benton, Mark Holden, Mark Preston, Mark Richardson, Martin Lane, Martin Panak, Martin Stow, Michel Annink, Mike Barnato, Mike Brown, Mike Tyler, Nahal Mehran, Nicola Quirk, Nigel Ayers, Oscar Alting, Patrick Blott, Patrick Brosnan, Paul Birt, Paul Fenny,

Paul Lowing, Peter Desmond, Peter Lewis Jones, Phil Ranson, Rama Venchard, Rebecca Crallan, Reena Patel, Richard Gough, Richard Higginson, Richard Read, Richard Roberts, Richard Warren, Robert Power, Rod Hulme, Ron Welker, Roy Fletcher, Roy Knight, Sarah Amies, Sarah Krchnavy, Simon Lasky, Simon Ormston, Stephen Blakeman, Stephen Hughes, Stephen Walsh, Steve Kerzman, Steve Player, Steve Quinn, Steve Wesmiller, Thomas Herbert, Tim Goodwin, Vicky Raymer, Victoria Fafalios, Wayne Tantrum, William Roberts, and Zoe Keens.

I would also like to thank my clients, old and new, for the challenges, insights and opportunities that have so contributed to the thinking that has been the basis for this work; my family for putting up with my perverse grumpiness as I struggled to find the right combination of words to put down on the page; and Jonathan Hooker for my own initiation into the world of meeting design, and for his inspirational example to my early work in this area.

And finally, I thank God for the time to focus on this, for the sense of joy and excitement I felt while I was writing it, and for the insights that have found their way into both my understanding and the pages of this book.